With Tongues of Fire

With Tongues of Fire

Profiles in 20th-Century Hymn Writing

PAUL WESTERMEYER

Foreword by Martin E. Marty

CPH™
SAINT LOUIS

To Martin E. Marty
scholar, teacher, advisor,
fellow Christian singer,
with gratitude

Library of Congress Cataloging-in-Publication Data

Westermeyer, Paul, 1940–
    With tongues of fire : profiles in 20th century hymn writing / Paul Westermeyer.
        p.   cm.
    Includes bibliographical references.
    ISBN 0-570-01349-6
    1. Hymn writers—United States—Interviews. 2. Hymn writers—Great Britain—
Interviews. 3. Hymns, English—History and criticism. 4. Hymns, English—United
States—History and criticism.
I. Title.
BV325.W47   1995
264'.2'097309045—dc20

95-17459

1 2 3 4 5 6 7 8 9 10   04 03 02 01 00 99 98 97 96 95

Contents

Foreword

The author of the play, performed so long ago, was certainly no Pulitzer Prizewinner. She could not have gotten the work produced even by a small high school drama club. Certainly the "one-acter" was not a feminist expression, though only women were in it. But, cursed or blessed with a cluttered mental attic, full of antique recall from a depression and drought childhood in Nebraska, I recall the little play better than many Pulitzers and all high school plays I've seen since.

Staged on an improvised platform made up of planks on saw horses, much like the "pews" on which the audience, a.k.a. congregation, sat on a festival summer Sunday afternoon, the play held our attention. We waited through it, itching to spend the nickel that was the customary parental bribe. Lures like that nickel helped us look forward to churchly entertainments in the days, pre-television, when such simplicities could still capture children's imaginations.

Nothing of what was said that afternoon sticks in my mind. I think the actresses spent much of the time in the one-acter drinking tea. What the cast wore does remain vivid in memory: the characters, probably of high school age, were dressed Victorianly, perhaps in clothes unmothballed from their grandmothers' trunks. (The Victorian Age had ended only about 35 years before the staging.) Now, to the point of all this scene-setting:

The unlikely heroine of this playlet was Catherine Winkworth. No, she was not a poet with a dramatic life like that of Elizabeth Barrett Browning or Christina Rossetti. Nor was she a hymn writer; I'd be tempted to say "*even* a hymn writer," were this not a book designed to show that hymn writers are important. She was a mere translator, as if practitioners of that art could ever be "mere." Her name is familiar among hymn singers who bother to read the fine print above or below the songs they sing. In fact, Winkworth merits 30 index references, the second-most of any one, in the hymnal we use weekly. Her translations hold up well, even better, to my taste, than those by "Catherine Winkworth, *alt.,*" "alt." referring to some committee member who was assigned to de-Victorianize her rendition, in order to make it more palatable and less authentic for our time.

Since the details of the old play plot were beyond my mental summonings, I cheated and looked for "Winkworth, Catherine (1829–78)" in tomes on the wall of encyclopedias, including dictionaries of Christianity, that loom behind my back as I type. Most did not mention her, but finally she turned up: a Manchesterian Winkworth she was, and, enjoy this: "She was a pioneer in women's higher education, a founder of Clifton High School, and she prepared the ground for the establishment of the University College at Bristol." Could it have been that the young women on stage that Sunday long ago, women including a couple of cousins of mine, were proto-feminists? Yes. They probably were. Being allowed to "move to town" to get into high school was beyond the range of many in such a rural congregation in the 1930s; the hunger for learning and self-expression, however, was there.

Again to the point: Winkworth published over 300 hymns in *Lyra Germanica,* 1855–58, and *The Chorale Book for England* (1863). Note also that she produced a biographical *Christian Singers of Germany* in 1869. I hope to find it in our university library's rare book section. This one would no doubt be rare as a result of its having been a popular book, one that had been bought and used and worn; few of such books would survive the centuries. Note, now, the relevance of all this lead-in to the book at hand, Paul Westermeyer's book of interviews, biographies, and hymnographies from which I am keeping you too long.

Such stage-setting is much to the point, I assume, given the fact that in our contemporary world this counterpart book to Winkworth's, one that could have been titled *Christian Singers of America and England and Other Parts,* needs some introducing. Not that we are so secularly beyond the scope of hymnsinging that this project is irrelevant. Nor even that we are in a period of dwindling productivity toward hymnlessness. I was surprised and happy to read on these pages that Paul Westermeyer and some of his cast think of ours as a fertile period for new hymn-writing. But it happens that hymns do not make Top 40 Charts. Good ones don't survive the current Christian obsession with the kind of "praise songs" that imitate bad Broadway or Country or good music forms. And those that *do* transcend the boundaries of mediocrity tend to come to us anonymously.

Though I am on the side of those who want to help hymn writers become anonymous, let me recognize that few lives on these pages are dramatic, or, if they are, the dramatic part is not relevant to the interviewer or interviewees. These are craft people who go about their craft with a sense of vocation, discipline, and dedication. As I read the long lists of hymns appendixed to these biographies, it struck me that only a small percentage have made their way into the contemporary canon, and one can assume that even fewer will be sung through the ages. On gloomy days, given the decline in taste in these market-oriented worship times, one has to hope that real hymns will be sung at all in that future. I write in the expectation that hymnody will survive (see below).

This little book, modest in design, should in its quiet way help stimulate curiosity about the hymn-writing and publishing impulse. I was struck as so often I am in the context of hymnodists by the diversity in the cast of this book's characters. It is often said that the hymnal is the most ecumenical achievement of the modern church, of all modern churches. I have heard fundamentalists sing hymns by modernists like Harry Emerson Fosdick, preachers they would never allow near their pulpits, and perhaps souls that they would not accept as those of fellow-pilgrims. There seems to be no single plot, no pattern of upbringing or schooling, no chart of professional routes to the calling of hymn writer. Each responds distinctively to the call she or he hears.

Those who have sung hymns by these authors will find their own rewards. Though not, for the moment, engaging in the typical author's ego-serving vice of looking for my own name in the index, I had the surprising thrill of seeing that Jaroslav Vajda, one of the subjects here, lists Christian thinkers who have had some influence on him, and found myself in that list. This foreword gives me the opportunity to say, even as I hope to speak for thousands, that *you* folks, you interviewees and biographees, and you, Paul Westermeyer, interviewer and biographer, have influenced us and can do more so with this new instrument in our hands.

Long after most essays of theologians in our day are forgotten, we and our heirs will be singing at least some of your work. This book should help inform that heritage. Before it becomes a rare book, it should move the singing church. And when it does become a rare book, let it give scholars of the future a chance to see that the craft of the hymnodist survived a period in which distraction, mediocrity, and banality were constant threats.

Soli Deo Gloria!

MARTIN E. MARTY

Publisher's Foreword

As an American theologian has suggested, one can tell more about a church body by listening to the songs it sings than by looking at its official documents. If hymn writers are faithful to their own Christian belief, then it follows that an examination of 20th-century hymn writing should reveal a great deal of the state of the church—its pressures, concerns, and triumphs. Paul Westermeyer (*The Church Musician*) leads us on an impressive and thought-provoking journey by examining the distinctive thrusts of hymn writing in the latter part of this century and through interviews with some of the poets themselves as well as with others who are influential in this vital part of parish life. Some of the viewpoints expressed in the interviews as well as within the hymns themselves will not be embraced by all denominations. Indeed, as a church body that regards the Scriptures as the inerrant Word of God and subscribes to the Lutheran Confessions, The Lutheran Church—Missouri Synod "believes, teaches, and confesses" that 1) Jesus Christ is the only way to salvation; 2) terminology describing the triune God should reflect biblical theology, including gender-specific language; 3) Scripture restricts ordination to the pastoral office to men; and 4) these and other doctrinal issues are of consequence for the ongoing life of the church. Nevertheless, the resulting profile will be of interest to all those who care deeply about the state of arts in the church in these days and will speak especially to the hearts of those who yearn for an expression of faith that is at once literate, substantive, contemporary, comprehensive, unafraid of Truth, and which fervently confesses the Hope which does not disappoint.

The Publisher

Acknowledgments

Chapter 1 is a revised version of a portion of a longer article, "Twentieth Century American Hymnody and Church Music," *New Dimensions in American Religious History: Essays in Honor of Martin E. Marty,* ed. Jay P. Dolan and James P. Wind (Grand Rapids: William B. Eerdmans Publishing Company, 1993), pp. 175–207. Used by permission.

The biographical sketch of Martin Franzmann found in Chapter 5 relies on *Thy Strong Word: The Enduring Legacy of Martin Franzmann* by Richard N. Brinkley (St. Louis: Concordia Publishing House, 1993), pp. 13–33.

The publisher also gratefully acknowledges the various publishers who granted permission for the inclusion of the selected hymn texts.

CHAPTER 1

Twentieth-Century English Hymnody in the United States

Hymnody in some fashion or other has accompanied the Christian church throughout its entire history. Psalms are embedded in the Old Testament, canticles (such as the songs of Mary and Simeon) in the New. Both were the birthright and practice of the early church which, in its Greek-speaking form, created more hymns. Ambrose, fourth-century bishop of Milan, generated an infusion of church song into Latin, as the 16th-century reformer Martin Luther did into German. French and English metrical psalms characterized Calvinists and Anglicans. Hymnic pieces called "sequences" were produced in profusion in the medieval period, and hymn writers such as Watts and Wesley dominated the period after the Reformation. Augustine in fifth-century North Africa represents all the bishops and writers who have noted the importance of hymnody. Translators such as Catherine Winkworth and John Mason Neale in 19th-century England stand for all those who have transferred the church's hymnic treasures from one language and culture to another. In short, by the time the 20th century arrived, the church's repertoire of hymns was vast, and many had realized how valuable that was.

Hymn singing has been a part of almost all 20th-century Christian groups in the United States. Most of the time hymnals have been used by them. Hymnals have been edited and published throughout this century. The Hymn Society in America and Canada has increased in membership and even publishes a quarterly journal of congregational song, *The Hymn*. There have been so many publications and so much activity that, at first glance, it all seems unwieldy. But it does have a shape.

At the beginning of the 20th century, hymnody in the United States was driven by three forces: 1) an ecumenical and historic breadth, 2) gospel hymnody, and 3) social concerns. The first two of these have symbolic dates prior to the 20th century, in 1895, and a call for the third came a little later. In expanded versions these forces continued throughout the century, with the second two gradually encompassed in the net of the first.

1) The denominational hymnals, though they are widely dispersed, broadly organize themselves into three clusters, around the early, middle, and end of the century. *The Presbyterian Hymnal* which Louis Benson (1855–1930) edited in 1895[1] (revised in 1911 and supplemented in 1917), the Episcopal *Hymnal* of 1916[2] in which Winfred Douglas (1867–1944) had a hand, and the Lutheran *Common Service Book* of 1917[3] of which Luther D. Reed (1873–1972) was a primary editor, represent the first cluster. The Episcopal *Hymnal 1940*[4], which Winfred Douglas edited, and many other denominational hymnals on either side of it, such as *The Lutheran Hymnal*[5], represent the second. The third cluster begins in 1978 with the *Lutheran Book of Worship*.[6] This cluster is still growing. Its most recent additions were published by the Mennonites and Brethren[7] in 1992, *Christian Worship* from the Wisconsin Synod Lutherans in 1993[8], and the United Church of Christ, the Moravians, and the Christian Church (Disciples of Christ) in 1995[9].

The major denominational hymnals of the 20th century have been influenced by an increasingly inclusive ecumenical and historical breadth. The hymnals at the beginning of the century were tinged with Victorian sentiments, ("From Greenland's Icy Mountains," "Onward Christian Soldiers") as one might expect, but essentially they were controlled by the ecumenical hymnic activity which had been begun in the 19th century. The English hymnal called *Hymns Ancient and Modern* of 1861—which brought together a broad ecumenical cross section of hymns from the entire history of the Christian church—was their model. This influence was felt even where one might not expect it, for example by the Baptists in *Sursum Corda* of 1898[10] which E. H. Johnson edited.

2) Gospel hymnody challenged the church's broader historic hymnic consciousness. The Dwight Moody-Ira Sankey campaigns in the last quarter of the 19th century produced a body of hymnody which was collected in 1895 in *Gospel Hymns Nos. 1 to 6 Complete.*[11] The music of that collection contained cheery compound triple and dotted rhythms, enticing mild chromaticism, the almost exclusive use of major keys rather than minor ones, and a lack of dissonance or musical argument to create tension. It developed into the even lighter, semi-sacred, and more commercial music of the Billy Sunday era after the turn of the century, such as "His Eye Is on the Sparrow" and "Ivory Palaces" from Charles Alexander's collections, Ina Ogden's "Brighten the Corner Where You Are," and George Bernard's "The Old Rugged Cross." It often took over Sunday schools altogether and made inroads into mainstream Protestant services as well. Sometimes songs in this style virtually replaced an entire hymnic heritage, at least in the Sunday school, if not beyond, as in the case of the German Evangelical Synod of North America (the denomination the influential theologians Richard and Reinhold Niebuhr came from) which in its *Elmhurst Hymnal* gave up its German chorales.[12] Independent publishers ground out pamphlets of gospel hymnody in great profusion.

3) The third force can be identified with a call by Walter Rauschenbusch for a hymnody associated with the social gospel. (This popular movement, which diminished in the 1930s, attempted to renew society by bringing in the kingdom of God and emphasized Jesus as example at the expense of Jesus as redeemer and conqueror of sin and death.) In his *Evangeliums-Lieder* of 1891[13] Rauschenbusch himself had translated Ira Sankey's gospel hymns into German, but, after the turn of the century, he attacked Christian hymnody generally and gospel hymnody specifically because it avoided service to humanity and postponed corrections of social ills to a future life.[14] He argued for a social gospel hymnody that would "voice the new social enthusiasms."[15] His cry found expression in a couple publications—Henry Sloane Coffin's *Hymns of the Kingdom of God*[16] and Mabel Mussey's *Social Hymns of Brotherhood and Aspiration.*[17] The challenge of its message, the task of creating new hymns, and the lack of gospel hymnody's enticements combined to keep social gospel hymnody from being a strong force or exert-

ing a large popular appeal. Hymns with societal themes were not absent from the period,[18] but they did not have the proportions or attractions of gospel hymnody.

Both societal concerns and gospel hymnody were gradually felt in denominational hymnals. For example, the Presbyterian hymnal of 1895 which Benson edited was "virtually free of gospel hymnody, tipping its hat barely in that direction with the inclusion of 'He Leadeth Me' and 'I Love to Tell the Story.'"[19] Benson's revision in 1911, however, included more hymns with a social emphasis,[20] and, just before the Anglican chants at the back of the book, a section of twenty-nine hymns headed "Evangelistic Services" was added. The Southern Presbyterians were influenced even more by gospel hymnody.[21]

This should not be understood to mean that denominations jettisoned their own hymnic traditions. Though there were exceptions, such as Presbyterians continuing to give up their heritage of metrical psalms or the German Evangelical Synod of North America giving up its chorales, as a general rule American denominations in the 20th century did not deny their individual traditions; instead, they continued to combine them with a cross section of other hymnic materials, adapted to their own idioms and confessional postures. *The Hymnal 1940* of the Episcopal Church, a classic production, best illustrates this pattern, but a spate of publications by other denominations up through the *Pilgrim Hymnal*[22] and *Service Book and Hymnal* of 1958[23] point to the same general flow.

The stretch from the Presbyterian hymnal in 1895 through the books just mentioned in 1958 could be described positively as a period when successive hymnal revisions developed steadily in ecumenical and historic breadth. Negatively, however, it could be said to consist "of a frozen repertory reshaped according to denominational needs."[24] The 1960s changed that.

The 1960s fostered what has come to be known as a hymn explosion. It began in Scotland, in response to a perennial cry of the period that "nobody's getting down to writing the hymns for our time."[25] With Erik Routley as the catalyst, meetings were held between 1961 and 1969 at the Scottish Churches House in Dunblane.[26] The participants included clergy, poets, musicians, teachers, and scholars who discussed hymnody seriously in relation to the present, and then produced texts and music which were published as *Dunblane Praises* and *New Songs for the Church*.

There was no comparable meeting in the 1960s on this side of the Atlantic, but publications such as *Songs for Today*,[27]: *Hymns for Now*,[28] and the *Hymnal for Young Christians*[29] gave voice to the same need for new paths.

This ferment created a whole body of new English hymns, largely by the writers who are interviewed in this book. From England we have the hymns of Fred Pratt Green, Timothy Dudley-Smith, Fred Kaan, and Brian Wren which made their way to the United States and Canada. Thomas H. Troeger, Jaroslav Vajda, and Carl Daw represent writers from the United States. Sylvia Dunstan stands for the Canadian stream. The hymns of these authors run a wide gamut, from the social passion of Brian Wren to the thick imagery of Thomas Troeger to the brief, evocative phrases of Jaroslav Vajda.

The ferment not only created texts. It and the new texts themselves stimulated new tunes and harmonizations. Calvin Hampton took old hymn texts and wrote new tunes for them, often with complex accompaniments. Carol Doran and Thomas Troeger collaborated on their creations. Doran has written tunes and harmonizations in songlike contemporary idioms that are consciously wedded to specific texts. Carl Schalk has written remarkably singable tunes, even for the unrhymed texts of Jaroslav Vajda which would seem to resist such settings.

This was indeed an explosion, but new texts and tunes tell only part of the story. In addition to the new, the century's high level historical momentum toward increasing ecumenical breadth resulted in hymnals picking up more of the old as well as the new. The white southern spirituals that George Pullen Jackson[30] had researched and black spirituals were included. "Folk" and "popular" idioms were added. Hispanic, Asian, and African hymns were increasingly sought. There was also a revival of psalm singing, not only of metrical psalms, but of prose chant versions as well.

With all of this, elements of gospel hymnody became more accessible to some who had earlier rejected it, and elements of the more historic repertoire became accessible to some who had earlier rejected it. The cleavages were not resolved, but gradually portions of the repertoire of gospel songs were being folded into the broader context of the church's hymnody.

That does not exhaust the story. Hymn explosions signal reformations or revolutions. This one was no exception. Hymnody prior to 1960 was not immune to the world around it. The temperance movement had its temperance hymnody.[31] The Episcopal hymnal of 1916 and the 1917 supplement to the 1895 Presbyterian hymnal "reflected the fact that the nation was at war;"[32] both hymnals included Rudyard Kipling's "God of Our Fathers, Known of Old," Francis Scott Key's "O Say Can You See," and Julia Ward Howe's "Mine Eyes Have Seen the Glory of the Coming of the Lord."[33] The editors of the Episcopal hymnal in 1916, included several of the best chorales, but because of war-time animosity against Germany, felt it necessary to camouflage them with English names: HERZLICH TUT MICH VERLANGEN became PASSION CHORALE. *The Hymnal 1940* continued this practice.[34] The rejection of their chorales by the Evangelical Synod of North America was due, at least in part, to the same anti-German fervor.

Hymnals prior to 1960 were not without their hymns or even sections on brotherhood, obedience, service, and love, but they also, like the products of every culture, reflected the period's blind spots. Jon Michael Spencer has pointed out the "liberative lag" in black Protestant hymnody and in white Protestant hymnody as a counterpart of white supremacy.[35] The two were mirror images of one another: neither group saw, for example, the degradation of Africa in "From Greenlands Icy Mountains" or the degradation of the African or African-American in "Wash Me and I Shall Be Whiter Than Snow;" or, if they saw, they could not perceive what such texts did to them or to their brothers and sisters in the other race; or, if they perceived, they could not change the situation.

The 1960s and beyond no doubt have their own blind spots which future historians will see better than we. But the ruptures of the 1960s—the Second Vatican Council; the assassinations of Jack Kennedy, Robert Kennedy, and Martin Luther King, Jr.; the racial conflicts and riots that followed; the Vietnam War and its aftermath—created a new world in which past blind spots suddenly became eye sores. A new and conscious response to the culture took shape. While not the optimistic social gospel that Rauschenbusch might have had in mind, it was a social consciousness nonetheless, though postponed to the end of the century and chastened by its horrors.

Sometimes the new hymn writing addressed social issues head on, as Rauschenbusch presumably would have liked. But a new consciousness also raised questions about language itself. At least three broad issues emerged. First, King James English with "thee," "thy," and "vouchsafe" seemed outdated, and new earthen vessels in 20th-century English seemed required. Second, the nature of language in relation to justice and peace was examined. How did the words of a hymn program the singers to perceive justice? Did the generic use of the male pronoun discriminate against women? Did language about the deaf and dumb match the injustice of washing blacks white? Did militaristic hymns program the singers to violence or idolatrous tribal persuasions? Third, the nature of poetry and especially hymnic poetry was considered, at a time when there was little or no consensus about what "good" poetry or art or music or architecture might be.[36]

These issues forced hymnal editors not only to choose from an overwhelming variety and number of texts and tunes, in and out of their own traditions, but also to decide about complex questions such as these: How much updating and changing of historic texts is advisable? Can a generic male pronoun ever be used with reference to humanity? What about male pronouns with reference to God? What happens to the poetry or the "rights" of a dead poet when changes are made? To what extent do the texts belong to the community once they leave the hands of the poet? What possible harm can come from editors changing what is in people's memory banks?

The momentum of hymnody should be noted here. Though hymnody does respond to the culture—and at points of shift, as in the 1960s and beyond, the influence is especially great—it also goes on as if it is independent of the culture. Most hymnal committees realized this and tried to stay in touch with their constituencies. The popularity of "Onward, Christian Soldiers," for example, got it into the Methodist hymnal of 1989, against the better judgment of many Methodists on and off the committee.

Lutheran Book of Worship of 1978 was the first major response to the new situation. Virtually every denomination has followed its lead. Committees now working on hymnals are still dealing with the same issues.

What the people sing assumes a community, in the case of the church, a congregation or choir. The music that is in the ear of a given community has included a wide variety of styles and performance practices: Old Regular Baptists in Blackey, Kentucky, with lined out hymns in an old New England style; Mennonites without instrumental accompaniment; Sacred Harp singers; Dutch Reformed metrical psalm singers; Norwegian Lutherans with a klokker; German Lutherans with rhythmic chorales; black congregations who utilized blue notes; rural congregations who sang with a fervor that included their own rhythmic and melodic twists; urban and suburban congregations who also sang with fervor, but in a more conventional 20th-century style; jazz masses at congregations in New York, Washington, Chicago, and other cities; Hispanic congregations with guitar and rhythm instruments; Southern Baptists with a song leader; Russian Orthodox choirs who, virtually from memory, sang 19th-century versions of Byzantine chant. Some of this could not be notated very easily, and some of it, when notated, did not sound in performance like the notation. Sometimes it was lackluster, lethargic, and downright awful (and so, it should be noted, was some music made by professionals!), but sometimes it has also been remarkable in both spirit and music.

As ethnic groups were amalgamated into the broader societal net and the nomadic culture of the century increased, in many cases these communities either disappeared or found themselves decimated. That gave rise to new communites of people with many different backgrounds and memories who were forced to fashion new songs. This painful struggle characterizes many groups at the end of the 20th century.

The musical leaders of these groups—organists or other instrumentalists, choir directors or song leaders—have included musicians with national reputations, for example, Mary Oyer of the Mennonites and Paul Manz of the Lutherans. But they have also included countless others who are anonymous beyond their local communities. Whether well-known or not, whether professional or amateur, those who were successful leaders sensed the musical and spiritual idiom of their people and were able to release, energize, and nourish it.

The hymn writers who form the next 10 chapters of this book represent the hymn explosion of the latter part of the 20th century. The seven who are alive are invariably named when the best hymn writers from the latter part of our century are discussed. These are not the only fine hymn writers among us, to be sure, but they have all made substantial contributions to hymnals of late 20th-century congregations.

The three who are deceased are in categories by themselves. Martin Franzmann wrote few hymns by comparison with the other writers, but several of them are of such high calibre that he needs to be included. Erik Routley is better characterized as a hymnnologist than a hymn writer, but his influence is so strong that it was deemed wise to include him as well. Like Franzmann, several of his hymns have also been widely used. Sylvia Dunstan died at the age of 38. She has not had the chance the other writers have had to receive wide circulation, but the quality of her hymn writing has already been appreciated by many and is likely to be discovered by many more.

In the following chapters we shall put the same general set of questions to each of the hymn writers (where possible). These are preceded by a biographical sketch, a partial list of publications, and a complete list of hymns at the time they were assembled. The writers are positioned alphabetically. The three who are dead will be given the chance to speak through previous writings. After these biographies, lists, and interviews a round-table discussion ensues gathering the insights of several influential people in the field of English-speaking congregational song. Finally I will attempt a general appraisal of all their observations and insights.

Notes

1. *The Hymnal Published by Authority of the General Assembly of the Presbyterian Church in the United States of America* (Philadelphia: Presbyterian Board of Publication and Sabbath-School Work), 1895.

2. *The Hymnal: As Authorized and Approved for Use by the General Convention of the Protestant Episcopal Church in the United States of America in the Year of Our Lord MCMXVI* (New York: Church Pension Fund), 1916 (first edition 1918).

3. *Common Service Book of the Lutheran Church: Authorized by the United Lutheran Church in America* (Philadelphia: Board of Publication of the United Lutheran Church in America), 1917.

4. *The Hymnal of the Protestant Episcopal Church in the United States of America 1940* (New York: Church Pension Fund), 1940 (published 1943).

5. *The Lutheran Hymnal: Authorized by the Synods Constituting the Evangelical Lutheran Synodical Conference of North America* (St. Louis: Concordia Publishing House), 1941.

6. *Lutheran Book of Worship* (Minneapolis: Augsburg Publishing House), 1978.

7. *Hymnal: A Worship Book Prepared by Churches in the Believers Church Tradition* (Elgin: Brethren Press), 1992.

8. *Christian Worship: A Lutheran Hymnal* (Milwaukee: Northwestern Publishing House), 1993.

9. *The New Century Hymnal* (Cleveland: The Pilgrim Press, 1995), *Moravian Book of Worship* (Bethlehem: Moravian Church in America, 1995), and *Chalice Hymnal* (St. Louis: Chalice Press, 1995).

10. *Sursum Corda: A Book of Praise,* ed. E. H. Johnson (Philadelphia: American Baptist Publication Society), 1898.

11. Ira Sankey, et al., *Gospel Hymns Nos. 1 to 6 Complete* (New York: Da Capo Press, 1972, unabridged republication of the "Excelsior Edition," published originally in 1895).

12. *Elmhurst Hymnal* (St. Louis: Eden Publishing House), 1921.

13. Walter Rauschenbusch, *Evangeliums-Lieder* (Cincinnati: John Church Company) 1891.

14. See Jon Michael Spencer, "Hymns of the Social Awakening: Walter Rauschenbusch and Social Gospel Hymnody," *The Hymn,* 40:2 (April, 1989), pp. 18–19.

15. Ibid, p. 19.

16. *Hymns for the Kingdom of God,* ed. Henry Sloane Coffin and Ambrose White Vernon (New York: A. S. Barnes), 1931 (first edition, 1909 or 1910).

17. *Social Hymns of Brotherhood and Aspiration,* ed. Mabel Hay Barrows Mussey (Boston: Universalist Publishing House), 1914.

18. See Paul Westermeyer, "Hymnody in the United States from the Civil War to World War I (1860–1916)," *The Hymnal 1982 Companion,* Volume I, ed. Raymond F. Glover (New York: The Church Hymnal Corporation, 1990.), pp. 447–51.

19. Morgan F. Simmons, "Hymnody: Its Place in Twentieth Century Presbyterianism" (unpublished typescript), p. 5.

20. Ibid, p. 9.

21. Ibid, p. 8.

22. *Pilgrim Hymnal* (Boston: Pilgrim Press), 1958.

23. *Service Book and Hymnal Authorized by the Lutheran Chuches Cooperating in the Commission on the Liturgy and Hymnal* (Minneapolis: Augsburg Publishing House), 1958.

24. Russell Schultz-Widmar, "Hymnody," *The Hymnal 1982 Companion,* p. 600.

25. Ian M. Fraser, "Beginnings at Dunblane," *Duty and Delight: Routley Remembered,* ed. Robin A. Leaver and James H. Litton (Carol Stream: Hope Publishing Company, 1985), p. 171.

26. Ibid. See the whole article for a chronicle of these meetings and the personalitites who shaped them.

27. *Songs for Today,* ed. Ewald Bash and John Ylvisaker (Minneapolis: American Lutheran Church), 1964.

28. *Hymns for Now: A Portfolio for Good, Bad, or Rotten Times* (Chicago: Walther League), 1967.

29. *Hymnal for Young Christians* (Chicago: Friends of the English Liturgy Church Publications), 1967.

30. See George Pullen Jackson, *White Spirituals in the Southern Uplands: The Story of the Fasola Folk, Their Songs, Singings, and "Buckwheat Notes"* (New York: Dover, 1965, reprint form 1933).

31. See Paul Westermeyer, "Chicago and Hymnody: A Tourist's Guide," *The Hymn,* 28:2 (April, 1977), p. 73.

32. Simmons, p. 10.

33. See William J. Reynolds, "The Hymnal 1940 and Its Era," *The Hymn,* 41:4 (October, 1990), p. 38.

34. Ibid.

35. Jon Michael Spencer, "Black Denominational Hymnody and Growth toward Religious and Racial Maturity," *The Hymn,* 41:4 (October 1990), pp. 41–45, especially p. 44.

36. John Cage, *Silence* (Cambridge: Massachusetts Institute of Technology, 1961) is a good illustration of the dilemma.

CHAPTER 2

Carl P. Daw, Jr.

Like the murmur of the dove's song,
like the challenge of her flight,
like the vigor of the wind's rush,
like the new flame's eager might:
    come, Holy Spirit, come.

To the members of Christ's Body,
to the branches of the Vine,
to the Church in faith assembled,
to her midst as gift and sign:
    come, Holy Spirit, come.

With the healing of division,
with the ceaseless voice of prayer,
with the power to love and witness,
with the peace beyond compare:
    come, Holy Spirit, come.

Biographical Sketch

Carl Pickens Daw, Jr., was born in 1944, the first of four children. At the time, his parents were living in Louisville where his father was in the last year of seminary, preparing to be a Baptist pastor. During World War II his father was a Navy chaplain and then became pastor of First Baptist Church in Newport, Tennessee. After that pastorate he went to Nashville to graduate school for five years and then to Murfreesboro, Tennessee, where Carl spent the rest of his boyhood before college. Carl is grateful for Tennessee's fine music programs as he was growing up. He studied both cello and piano.

Carl enrolled at Rice University and became an English major. He completed his B.A. in 1966, then went to the University of Virginia as a graduate student in English. He finished an M.A. in 1967 and a Ph.D. in 1970. His dissertation was titled "An Annotated Edition of Five Sermons by Jonathan Swift." During his graduate school years he became an Episcopalian (not, he says, a wrenching experience, since his father had considered doing the same thing). He also met his wife May Bates, a professional librarian and amateur musician. They were married in 1969.

Immediately after his doctorate was finished, Daw began teaching English at the College of William and Mary in Williamsburg, Virginia. He taught graduate classes, including a course about the effect of music on a text. For this course he used his record collection and also built a harpsichord to demonstrate Elizabethan lute songs which his wife sang while he played.

Feeling called to the priesthood, Daw left William and Mary in 1978 and went to the School of Theology at the University of the South in Sewanee, Tennessee. He met Marion Hatchett who was teaching there and was also the chair of the text committee for the Episcopal hymnal that was in preparation. Daw became a consultant member of the committee, and, in the process of working with the theology and language of hymns, began to write texts himself. His hymns have now appeared not only in the *Episcopal Hymnal 1982,* but in many other hymnals as well.

After graduation from seminary in 1981, Daw went to Petersburg, Virginia, where he was assistant rector of Christ and Grace Church for three years. Then, in 1984, he went to Storrs, Connecticut, as Vicar-Chaplain of St. Mark's Chapel at the University of Connecticut. In the 1988–89 academic year he also served as Lecturer in English at the University of Connecticut. In 1993 he and his wife moved to Aliquippa, Pennsylvania, to live with the Community of Celebration.

Daw is a member of many professional organizations related both to the academic and ecclesiastical communities. These include the Modern Language Association, the Association of Anglican Musicians, the Association of Diocesan Liturgy and Music Commissions, and the Hymn Society in the United States and Canada. He has served as Secretary and Chair of the Standing Committee on Church

Music of the Episcopal Church. And he has conducted numerous workshops about topics related to hymnody, liturgy, music, and spirituality.

Daw and his wife have one daughter, Elizabeth ("Eliza"), who was born in 1975.

Publications

"Approaches to Hymn Writing: II." *The Hymn,* 35:2 (April, 1984), 80–81.

"Are Church Musicians Called or Hired?: An example of the Tension Between Doctrine and Discipline." *Association of Anglican Musicians Newsletter* (November, 1987), 3.

"The Exegesis of Liturgical Space." *Open* (March, 1987), 1–11.

"An Interview with Carl Daw," by Harry Eskew. *The Hymn* 40:2 (April, 1989), 24–29.

"The Prophetic Potential of Liturgy and Music." *Open* (February, 1986), pp. 1–11. Reprinted in *Liturgy and Music* [Diocese of Los Angeles], no. 10 (February, 1987), pp. 1–12, and *St. Luke's Journal of Theology,* 33:2 (March, 1990), 103–18.

"Sermon at the Closing Eucharist of the 1988 AAM Conference." *Association of Anglican Church Musicians Newsletter* (July, 1988), 6–8.

"The Spirituality of Anglican Hymnody: A Twentieth-Century American Perspective." *A Companion to the Hymnal 1982,* Volume 1, ed. Raymond F. Glover. New York: Church Hymnal Corporation, 1991, pp. 7–12.

To Sing God's Praise: 18 Metrical Canticles. Carol Stream: Hope Publishing Company, 1992.

"Towards More Inclusive Hymnody." *Plumbline* 17:1 (February, 1989), 21–23.

A Year of Grace: Hymns for the Church Year. Carol Stream: Hope Publishing Company, 1990.

Hymns

As panting deer desire the waterbrooks
As we gather at your table

Be joyful in the Lord
Beside the streams of Babylon
Blessed be the God of Israel

Christ the Victorious, give to your servants
Come, Jesus, come Morning Star
"Come, Lazarus," the Savior called
Come, let us sing with joy to the Lord

For the coming of the Savior
For the life that you have given
For the splendor of creation
From God alone begotten
From heaven above I come to you

Gentle Joseph heard a warning
Glory to our boundless God
Glory to you, our faithful God
God is not lifted up
God of grace and God of laughter
God of the prophets, bless the prophets' heirs
God our Author and Creator
God the Spirit, guide and guardian
God's glory fills the heavens with hymns
God's Paschal Lamb is sacrificed for us

How shallow former shadows seem
How lovely is thy dwelling-place

Into Jerusalem Jesus rode

Let all creation bless the Lord
Let kings and prophets yield their name

CARL P. DAW, JR.

Like the murmur of the dove's song

Make straight in the desert a highway
Mark how the Lamb of God's self-offering
Messengers of God's own sending
My soul proclaims with wonder

Nova, nova. Ave fit ex Eva.
Now have you set your servant free, O Lord

O day of peace that dimly shines
O God in whom all life begins
O God of font and altar
O God, on whom we lost our hold
O God, who gives us life and breath
O Light whose splendor thrills and gladdens
O risen Christ, still wounded

Praise God, whose providential awkwardness

Restore in us, O God
Rise up and shine!

Seek the Lord, whose willing presence
Sing of Andrew, John's disciple
Sing of God made manifest
Sing to the Lord, who has vanquished the horse and the warrior
"Sleeper, wake!" A voice astounds us
Soaring Spirit, set us free
Sovereign Maker of all things
Splendor and honor, majesty and power
Surely it is God who saves me

The house of faith has many rooms
The Lord my shepherd guards me well

We have come at Christ's own bidding
We marvel at your mighty deeds
We praise you, O God, and acclaim you as Lord

What boundless love, O Carpenter of Nazareth
When God's time had ripened
When Thomas heard the strange report
Where charity and love increase
Wild and lone the prophet's voice
With the body that was broken
Wondrous God, more named than known

Interview

PW: *Could you summarize your theological viewpoint?*

CD: Probably the most important, central theme from which my hymns radiate is the mystery of God's grace and our human incapacity to anticipate or comprehend it. (A primary expression of this tension is "Praise God whose providential awkwardness," whose title—before I adopted the practice of identifying my texts by their first lines—was simply "Grace.") Because I understand the experiences of Christian community, corporate worship (especially as expressed in the Sacraments), the reading of Scripture, and daily living as being potential ways of encounter with God, these are the contexts through which I usually approach this recurring concern.

PW: *What do you hope to write in the future?*

CD: More psalm paraphrases, more explorations of biblical stories, more affirmations of human diversity, more affirmations of faithful questioning and searching.

PW: *Is there anything you now wish you had not written?*

CD: Not much, really; I'm not entirely comfortable now with some of the male pronouns for God I used 10 years ago, but I hesitate to try to revise texts that are already known and used. My chief regret is that many people don't know anything of mine but "Like the murmur of the dove's song."

PW: *How do you see the hymn functioning in worship?*

CD: With allowance for differences in particular traditions, I see worship as having four broad movements: gathering, celebrating (which includes elements of praising, meditating, and proclaiming), identifying with God and each other, and dismissing/sending forth. These four movements are somewhat analagous to Dix's fourfold shape of the Eucharist: taking, blessing, breaking, and giving. Indeed, via Karl Rahner's theology of "the Church as fundamental sacrament" there is a kind of concentric relationship between these two analyses. In any case, I believe that hymnody is vital in creating and maintaining such a cohesive shape in worship. For example, the opening hymn is an essential part of the gathering movement. If it is too introspective, too individualistic, too ready to send people out before they have gathered and worshiped (worse case scenario: "Lord, dismiss us with thy blessing" as the opening hymn), too unfamiliar, or in any other way unsuited to including the hearts and minds of the congregation, the possibility of that service bringing people closer to God and to each other is greatly diminished. Nor is the conclusion of the service any less crucial. Final hymns that are too self-congratulatory and too smug will not send people back into their lives with renewed vigor and Christian commitment. The middle hymns similarly help to provide connections between the spoken parts of the service and the experience of the congregation; what people sing is their "AMEN" to what is said.

PW: *How do you perceive your influence? Is it regional or broader than that?*

CD: At this point it is arguably national and ecumenical, and it is beginning to be international.

PW: *How do you see your work in relation to late 20th-century hymnody generally?*

CD: I think of myself very much in terms of trying to connect the awareness and sensibilities of a late 20th-century person with the fundamental affirmations and questions of the traditional Christian pilgrimage of faith.

PW: *What in the current hymnic scene gratifies you?*

CD: The sheer wealth of talent and energy being devoted to hymn writing these days is incredibly exciting.

PW: *Is there anything you find alarming?*

CD: The promulgation of praise choruses and other musical "junk food" that trivializes the spiritual significance of sacred song is most distressing.

PW: *What does the future of American/English hymnody hold?*
CD: I can't predict this.

PW: *What do you regard as the three (or two or one) most representative hymns you have written?*
CD: This is like trying to decide which of one's children has the strongest family resemblance! At the moment, at least, I regard "Praise God whose providential awkwardness," "Like the murmur of the dove's song," and "When God's time had ripened" as being particularly important to me.

PW: *How do you feel you have been treated by hymnal editors?*
CD: On the whole, editors have treated my texts well, but there are a few painful exceptions (which I'd rather not name). The chief irritations are adding capitalization for pronouns referring to God, adding capitalization at the beginning of each line, and adding punctuation inconsistent with my intention. All these intrude on the visual impression the text makes and therefore on its comprehension by the reader or singer.

PW: *What or who influenced you? Why do you write hymns?*
CD: I'm not able to identify any particular influence, though I am grateful for having begun to write hymns while serving on a hymnal committee which included the late F. Bland Tucker. I began writing hymns as part of the work of that committee, which led to various commissions for new texts. I now write out of a sense of vocation: that this is one of the ways God is calling me to use whatever gifts have been intrusted to me.

PW: *What process do you follow when writing?*
CD: There is so much variation here that I cannot discern any set pattern. Sometimes I am trying to paraphrase Scripture, or meditate on a biblical story. Sometimes I am trying to find new words for a specific tune. Sometimes I am wrestling with a problem of faith. Often I am trying to find a way to deal with a particular theme or situation that has been given to me by a commissioning body.

CARL P. DAW, JR.

1 When God's time had ripened
    Mary's womb bore fruit,
scion of the Godhead
    sprung from Jesse's root;
so the True Vine branches
    from the lily's stem,
the Rose without blemish
    blooms in Bethlehem.

2 More than mind can fathom,
    limit, or untwine,
this mysterious yoking,
    human and divine;
but what reason fetters,
    faith at length unlocks,
and wise hearts discover
    truth in paradox.

3 As the Bread of Heaven,
    that we might be fed,
chose a manger cradle
    in the House of Bread,
so has Life Eternal
    mingled in the womb
with our mortal nature
    to confound the tomb.

4 For this swaddled infant
    in a humble place
holds our hope of glory
    and our means of grace;
in the Love enfleshed here
    dawns the world's rebirth,
promise of salvation,
    pledge of peace on earth.

CHAPTER 3

Timothy Dudley-Smith

He comes to us as one unknown,
    a breath unseen, unheard;
as though within a heart of stone,
or shrivelled seed in darkness sown,
    a pulse of being stirred.

He comes when souls in silence lie
    and thoughts of day depart;
half-seen upon the inward eye,
a falling star across the sky
    of night within the heart.

He comes to us in sound of seas,
    the ocean's fume and foam;
yet small and still upon the breeze,
a wind that stirs the tops of trees,
    a voice to call us home.

He comes in love as once he came
    by flesh and blood and birth;
to bear within our mortal frame
a life, a death, a saving Name,
    for every child of earth.

He comes in truth when faith is grown;
    believed, obeyed, adored:
the Christ in all the Scriptures shown,
as yet unseen, but not unknown,
    our Saviour and our Lord.

Biographical Sketch

Timothy Dudley-Smith was born on December 26, 1926, in Manchester, England. He grew up in Derbyshire and attended his father's school until his father died when he was 11. At about this time he sensed the call to the ordained ministry which was reaffirmed as he grew older.

Dudley-Smith's father introduced him to poetry. Other teachers encouraged the interest. At Cambridge he wrote comic verse regularly and also began the small collection of Christian verse since published in *Lift Every Heart* (Hope Publishing Company). He received his B.A. in 1947, his M.A. in 1951, and was ordained a deacon in 1950 and a priest in 1951.

Between 1950 and 1953 he served as the Assistant Curate at St. Paul's Church, Northemberland Heath, on the edge of London. Between 1953 and 1955 he was Head of the Cambridge University Mission in Bermondsey and its Chaplain from 1955 to 1960. From 1955 to 1959 he started and edited *Crusade,* a popular Christian monthly.

In 1959 he married June Arlette MacDonald and went to work as Assistant Secretary of the Church Pastoral Aid Society, a home missionary society of the Church of England. While serving in this capacity, he and Michael Baughen—another member of the staff—worked together on *Youth Praise,* he as publisher, Baughen as editor and compiler. *Youth Praise* became *Youth Praise 1.* It was followed by *Youth Praise 2* to which Dudley-Smith contributed more of his own hymns. *Youth Praise 1* and *2* combined sold more than one million copies by 1973.

In 1965, when Dudley-Smith became Secretary to the Church Pastoral-Aid Society, he had to give up his publishing responsibilities, but he was able to contribute to a project Michael Baughen began—a collection of metrical psalms called *Psalm Praise.* He was living in Sevenoaks, a town in Kent from which he commuted to London. Many of his texts from this period are therefore marked "Sevenoaks."

In 1973 he became Archdeacon of Norwich. By this time he and his family had a small house in Cornwall which they used each year for their vacations. At this house, called Seacroft, Dudley-Smith has written many hymns. His schedule there made it possible for him to write at breakfast before the rest of the family was up, and again later in the afternoon. During the rest of the year he found it difficult to find time for writing hymns. When he became Bishop of Thetford in 1981, the pattern continued.

In January of 1992 Timothy Dudley-Smith retired and moved with his wife to Salisbury where she had lived before they were married. Their daughter Caroline is married to Dr. David Gill, a lecturer in classical archaeology at the University of Swansea, South Wales. Their younger daughter, Sarah, is married to the Rev. Giles Walter, Vicar of St. John's Church, Turnbridge Wells, Kent; and until recently curate and 'Minister to Students' at the Round Church, Cambridge. Their son James teaches Modern Languages at Canford School, Dorset.

Dudley-Smith has been Honorary Chaplain to the Bishop of Rochester, Examining Chaplain to the Bishop of Norwich, Commissary to two Archbishops of Sydney, Australia, President of the Evangelical Alliance, and President of the Church of England Evangelical Council and Anglican Evangelical Assembly. He is a life member of the Royal Commonwealth Society, the Friends of the Cambridge University Library, the National Book League, and the Hymn Society in the United States and Canada as well as a member of the Hymn Society of Great Britain and Ireland.

Publications

Lift Every Heart: Collected Hymns 1961–1983 and Some Early Poems. Carol Stream: Hope Publishing Company/London: Collins Liturgical Publications, 1984.

Praying with the English Hymn Writers. London: Society for the Promotion of Christian Knowledge, 1989.

Songs of Deliverance: 36 New Hymns Written Between 1984 and 1987. Carol Stream: Hope Publishing Company/London: Hodder & Stoughton, 1988.

A Voice of Singing: 36 New Hymns Written Between 1988 and 1992. Carol Stream: Hope Publishing Company/London: Hodder & Stoughton, 1988.

Hymns

A city radiant as a bride
A new song God has given
A purple robe, a crown of thorn
A song was heard at Christmas
A stone to be the lintel
Above the voices of the world around me
All flowers of garden, field and hill
All glory be to God on high
All my soul to God I raise
All our days we will bless the Lord
All shall be well!
Almighty Lord Most High draw near
An upper room with evening lamps ashine
And sleeps my Lord in silence yet
Approach with awe this holiest place
As for our world we lift our hearts in praise
As in that upper room you left your seat
As water to the thirsty
At Cana's wedding, long ago

Be present, Spirit of the Lord
Be strong in the Lord
Behold a broken world, we pray
Behold, as love made manifest
Beloved in Christ before our life began
Beyond all mortal praise
Bless the Lord as day departs
Bless the Lord, creation sings
Born by the Holy Spirit's breath
By loving hands the Lord is laid

Child of Mary, newly born
Child of the stable's secret birth
Chill of the nightfall
Christ be my leader by night as by day
Christ be the Lord of all our days
Christ from heaven's glory come

TIMOTHY DUDLEY-SMITH

Christ high-ascended, now in glory seated
Christ is come! Let earth adore him
Christ is risen as he said
Christ is the Bread of life indeed
Christ is the one who calls
Christ the way of life possess me
Christ who called disciples to him
Come and see where Jesus lay
Come, let us praise the Lord
Come now with awe, earth's ancient vigil keeping
Come, watch with us this Christmas night
Comfort and peace to every heart!

Dear Lord, who bore our weight of woe
Donkey plod and Mary ride
Draw near to God, whose steadfast love

Every heart its tribute pays
Eye has not seen, nor ear has heard
Exult, O morning stars aflame

Faithful vigil ended
Father, now behold us
Father of lights, who brought us birth
Father on high to whom we pray
Father who formed the family of man
Fill your hearts with joy and gladness
For peace with God above
Freely, for the love he bears us
From afar a cock is crowing
From all the wind's wide quarters
From life's bright dawn to eventide
From the Father's throne on high
From the night of ages waking
Faithful trees, the Spirit's sowing

Give thanks to God on high
Glory to God in the highest

God and Father, ever giving
God is King! The Lord is reigning
God is my great desire
God is not far, whose threefold mercies shine
God lies beyond us, throned in light resplendent
God of eternal grace
God of gods, we sound his praises
God of old, whom saints and sages
God whose love is everywhere
Good news of God above

Had he not loved us
He comes to us as one unknown
He walks among the golden lamps
Hear how the bells of Christmas play!
Heavenly hosts in ceaseless worship
Heaven's throne ascending
Here is the centre: star on distant star
Here within this house of prayer
High peaks and sunlit prairies
Holy child, how still you lie
How faint the stable-lantern's light
How great our God's majestic Name!
'How shall they hear,' who have not heard
Hush you, my baby

I lift my eyes
In endless exultation
In my hour of grief or need

Jesus is the Lord of the living
Jesus my breath, my life, my Lord
Jesus, Prince and Saviour

Let every child of earth that sleeping lies
Let hearts and voices blend
Let the earth acclaim him
Let us sing the God of glory

Light of the minds that know him
Lighten our darkness now the day is ended
Living Lord, our praise we render
Long before the world is waking
Look, Lord, in mercy as we pray
Lord Jesus, born a tiny child
Lord, as the day begins
Lord, for the gift of this new day
Lord, for the years your love has kept and guided
Lord, give us eyes to see
Lord God almighty, Father of all mercies
Lord, hear us as we pray
Lord Jesus, born a tiny child
Lord of our lives, our birth and breath
Lord of the church, we pray for our renewing
Lord, when the storms of life arise
Lord, who left the highest heaven

May the love of Christ enfold us
Mercy, blessing, favour, grace
My days of waiting ended

Name of all majesty
No temple now, no gift of price
No tramp of soldiers' marching feet
No weight of gold or silver
Not for tongues of heaven's angels
Not in lordly state and splendour
Not to us be glory given
Now is Christ risen from the dead
Now to the Lord we bring the child he gave us

O changeless Christ, for ever new
O child of Mary, hark to her
O Christ the King of glory
O Christ the same, through all our story's pages
O Christ, who taught on earth of old
O come to me, the Master said

O God of living light
O God who brought the light to birth
O God who shaped the starry skies
O God whose thoughts are not as ours
O Lord, yourself declare
O Lord, whose saving name
Open our eyes, O Lord, we pray
O Prince of peace whose promised birth
O Saviour Christ, beyond all price
Our God and Father bless
Our God eternal, reigning
Our Saviour Christ once knelt in prayer
Out of darkness let light shine!

Peace be yours and dreamless slumber
Praise be to Christ in whom we see
Praise the God of our salvation
Praise the Lord and bless his Name
Praise the Lord of heaven

Remember, Lord, the world you made

Safe in the shadow of the Lord
Saviour Christ
See, to us a child is born
Servants of the living Lord
'Set your troubled hearts at rest'
Sing a new song to the Lord
So the day dawn for me
Soft the evening shadows fall
Spirit of faith, by faith be mine
Spirit of God within me
Stars of heaven, clear and bright

Tell his praise in song and story
Tell out, my soul, the greatness of the Lord
Thankful of heart for days gone by
The best of gifts is ours

The church of God on earth, we come
The darkness turns to dawn
The everlasting Lord is King
The faithful are kept as the mountains
The God of grace is ours
The heavens are singing, are singing and praising
The king of glory comes to earth
The Lord in wisdom made the earth
The Lord is here!
The Lord made man, the scriptures tell
The love of Christ, who died for me
The pilgrim church of God
The shining stars unnumbered
The stars declare his glory
The will of God to mark my way
This cherished child of God's creation
This child from God above
This day above all days
Timeless love! We sing the story
To Christ our King in songs of praise
To God our great salvation
To God who gave the scriptures
To heathen dreams of human pride
To this our world of time and space

We believe in God the Father
We come as guests invited
We come with songs of blessing
We sing the Lord our light
We turn in faith to Christ the Lamb of God
We turn to Christ alone
We turn to Christ anew
What colors God has made
When the Spirit came
When he comes
When Jesus lived among us he came a child of earth
When Jesus taught by Galilee
When John baptized by Jordan's river

When the Lord in glory comes
When the way is hard to find
When to our world the Saviour came
Where do Christmas songs begin?
Who is Jesus? Friend of sinners
Who is there on this Easter morning
With undivided heart and ceaseless songs
Within a crib my Saviour lay
Within the love of God I hide

Your voices raise to the Father's praise

Discontinued Texts

Father, we bring you

Merciful and gracious be

O God, our Father and our King
O thank the Lord for he is good
Our God has turned to his people

Interview

PW: Could you give some sense of your theological stance?
TDS: I stand squarely in the evangelical tradition of the Church of England—and towards the conservative end of that tradition. This means that I hold a high view of the authority of Scripture, and that from the inwardness of true religion and the search for personal holiness there comes Christian social concern for love and justice towards my neighbor.

PW: What does the future hold for your writing?
TDS: I hope to write further hymn texts and perhaps librettos for cantatas, etc. I wrote a short one for school choir and orchestra a few years ago, published in the United Kingdom by Stainer & Bell, entitled "Stone on Stone." And I have agreed to start work on a biography of the Rev. J. R. W. Stott, the most influential Anglican of this century, as I believe.

PW: *What do you wish you had not written?*

TDS: I don't know about "wishing I had not written them," but I no longer list among my texts the following: "Father, We Bring You" which is too tied to the particular occasion for which it was written; "Merciful and Gracious Be" which is not untrue to Psalm 56, but I am not happy about putting into the mouth of Christian congregations in the present day the last three lines of stanza 2; "O God, Our Father and Our King" which is just not good enough; "O Thank the Lord for He Is Good" which was experimental in using assonance in place of rhyme and seems facile; and "Our God Has Turned to His People" which, though it still has a continuing demand, seems like a jingle and unworthy of the Scriptural original, again perhaps facile. (These are listed in *Lift Every Heart,* Appendix 6, p. 289.) It is a tricky business to select texts which seem to fall short of a standard one sets oneself. In some moods, very little of what I have written would pass such a test.

PW: *How do you see the hymn functioning in worship?*

TDS: I believe that Erik Routley understood hymnody more than most; and I go along with his threefold purpose of hymnody in worship: "codifying doctrine, unifying the body, worshiping God."

PW: *How do you see your influence? Is it regional or more broad than that?*

TDS: I don't know about influence, but certainly my texts are published and sung in Australia, India, New Zealand, Africa, China (in English and in translation), Canada, the United Kingdom, and the United States.

PW: *How do you see your work in relation to late 20th-century hymnody generally?*

TDS: Perhaps as something of a bridge, to help those wedded to traditional hymnody (as I am myself) to move as painlessly as possible into modern English (no archaisms, etc.) and contemporary style, without losing some sense of dignity in the worship of God, and the need for the hymn to relate the objective truths of the faith with our subjective response. One can pick up a certain feel for this in Christopher Idle's article

"Tell Out the Greatness of the Lord: The Hymns of Timothy Dudley-Smith," *Evangelicals Now* (January 1992).

PW: *What in the current hymnic scene gratifies you?*

TDS: The renewed interest in hymnody and the growing awareness (as I believe) that a good hymn tune needs a good text.

PW: *Is there anything you find alarming?*

TDS: The apparent belief that anyone with a guitar can dash off a "worship song" fit to be sung by a congregation to almighty God, without effort, consultation, or revision—and often without grammar, syntax, meter, or rhyme either!

PW: *What do you think the future of American/English hymnody holds?*

TDS: Who knows? But I believe it is worth working hard to try to see that our *heritage* of hymnody is passed on to a new generation, and that they are not left to rely on the inspiration of their (or our) contemporaries.

PW: *What do you regard as the three (or two or one) most representative hymns you have written?*

TDS: People sometimes ask if I have a favorite, and I am always pleased when I can say that it is the one written most recently. But I do like "He Comes to Us as One Unknown" (*Lift Every Heart,* p. 89), "Stars of Heaven" (*Lift Every Heart,* p. 142), and "Lord of Our Lives, Our Birth and Breath" (*A Voice of Singing,* p. 26, which I would be happy to have sung at my funeral).

PW: *How do you feel you have been treated by hymnal editors?*

TDS: With few exceptions, I have been very well treated, notably, of course, in the United States by Hope Publishing Company, where George Shorney has become a valued friend. I decline editorial requests to make changes in the interests of inclusive language of *deity,* and remonstrate gently with editors who request this, but to little avail, I believe.

PW: *What or who influenced you? Why do you write hymns?*

TDS: I write hymns because God gives me something to say and a way to say it, because I enjoy it (in spite of the griefs and frustrations and hang-ups), and because of the parable of the talents. Poets who have influenced me by their writing include A. E. Housman, John Betjeman, and Walter de la Mare.

PW: *What processes do you follow when writing a hymn?*
TDS: See *Lift Every Heart,* pp. 31–42.

(Author's note: Here Timothy Dudley-Smith attempts to give a detailed look at the compositional process that produced "O Changeless Christ." From his manuscript book he culled out the text and the notes he made about it in the summer of 1981. He leads the reader through a whole series of transformations, from meter to rhymes to the order of stanzas. This lengthy account cannot be summarized. Suffice it to say the work is painstakingly careful and thoughtful.)

PW: *Do you want to add anything?*
TDS: I wonder about the variety of meters of my hymns and how that compares with the variety of meters in a typical hymnal. I also have a fondness for Christmas. My childhood Christmases were happy times, as were our family ones ever since our family started. My eldest child and I both have birthdays on December 26. So I find Christmas, for all its commercialism and worldliness, is still a special time. To keep in touch with distant friends we send a family Christmas card. I have now written a Christmas hymn or poem for 26 of these and hope to continue the tradition. Twenty-six texts on the theme of Christmas, out of a total of about 200, is quite a high proportion.

> Stars of heaven, clear and bright,
> shine upon this Christmas night.
> Vaster far than midnight skies
> are its timeless mysteries.
> Trampled earth and stable floor
> lift the heart to heaven's door—
> God has sent to us his Son,
> earth and heaven meet as one.
>
> Sleepy sounds of beast and byre
> mingle with the angel choir.
> Highest heaven bends in awe
> where he lies amid the straw,

whom from light eternal came
aureoled in candle-flame—
>God has sent to us his Son,
>earth and heaven meet as one.

Wide-eyed shepherds mutely gaze
at the child whom angels praise.
Threefold gifts the wise men bring,
to the infant priest and king:
to the Lord immortal, myrrh
for an earthly sepulchre—
>God has sent to us his Son,
>earth and heaven meet as one.

Heaven of heavens hails his birth,
King of glory, child of earth,
born in flesh to reign on high,
Prince of life to bleed and die.
Throned on Mary's lap he lies,
Lord of all eternities—
>God has sent to us his Son,
>earth and heaven meet as one.

"Glory be to God on high,
peace on earth," the angels cry.
Ancient enmities at rest,
ransomed, reconciled and blest,
in the peace of Christ we come,
come we joyful, come we home—
>God has sent to us his Son,
>earth and heaven meet as one.

CHAPTER 4

Sylvia Dunstan

You, Lord, are both Lamb and Shepherd.
      You, Lord, are both prince and slave.
You, peace-maker and sword-bringer
      of the way you took and gave.
You, the everlasting instant;
      You, whom we both scorn and crave.

Clothed in light upon the mountain,
      stripped of might upon the cross,
      shining in eternal glory,
      beggar'd by a soldier's toss,
You, the everlasting instant;
You who are both gift and cost.

You, who walk each day beside us,
      sit in power at God's side.
You, who preach a way that's narrow,
      have a love that reaches wide.
You, the everlasting instant;
      You, who are our pilgrim guide.

Worthy is our earthly Jesus!
      Worthy is our cosmic Christ!
Worthy your defeat and victory.
      Worthy still your peace and strife.
You, the everlasting instant;
      You, who are our death and life.

Biographical Sketch

(Author's note: This sketch was assembled largely from information graciously supplied by Judith Tansley.)

Sylvia Dunstan (1955–93) was born in Simcoe, Ontario, Canada, on May 26, 1955, and was reared by her grandparents who had Methodist and Salvation Army backgrounds. Church was important for them. Their Methodist heritage made its mark in part of the name "Jonathan Wesley Puzzle"—which Sylvia gave to her first teddy bear. Active as a young person in St. James United Church, she also attended high school in Simcoe.

For her undergraduate work Dunstan went to York University in Toronto. Her major was history. She graduated with a B.A. in 1976, then went on to Emmanuel College at the University of Toronto. There she received her M.Div. in 1980 and was also ordained in the United Church of Canada in the same year. Six years later she received the Th.M., also from Emmanuel College.

For her first pastoral charge Dunstan went to Alma-Albert in New Brunswick, a two-point responsibility. She returned to Ontario where she became duty chaplain of a maximum security jail in Whitby. Simultaneously she edited the United Church's worship publication called "Gathering." Before her death she served as interim pastor at the Malvern-Emmanuel pastoral charge in Scarborough, a suburb of Toronto.

Dunstan spent a goodly portion of her time doing committee work for the United Church of Canada. She was a member of the Education Student Committee, the group in the United Church which interviews candidates for ministry. She served as a member of the Agenda Planning Committee for both local and national assemblies. As a member of the national Worship Committee, she was co-author and editor of a number of liturgies, including A Sunday Liturgy, Baptism, and Renewal of Baptismal Faith. The Prayer of Thanksgiving over water was her writing.

In addition to her other work, she sometimes taught with Alan Barthel at Emmanuel College. He prodded her to write hymns. She had written poetry from school days onward, and Barthel's pressuring was one of the influences that led to its taking hymnic shape. At the time of her death she had written about half of a complete metrical psalter in addition to hymns.

Endowed with a fine voice, Dunstan sang and played the guitar both at church services and on other occasions. She was most herself, however, when she presided "at the table." She loved the liturgy. When she got sick, not only was a care team quickly assembled around her, but each night a small gathering of the church led by a member of the clergy celebrated communion with her.

In addition to being a fine cook, a connoisseur of fine wines, and a lover of Renaissance music and jazz, books were one of her passions. She had an extensive collection of hymnals (some first editions), liturgies, sermons, and many of Kierkegaard's works. Female poets and science fiction also interested her.

She did not like to fly, and she did not like doctors. In November of 1992, however, when she collapsed with what was presumed to be a heart attack, she was forced to go to the doctor. On March 21, 1993, an ultra-sound revealed cancer of the liver which by then had spread from the colon and metastasized. At the age of 38, on July 25, 1993, she died at home. She presided at her last service a little over a month earlier for the wedding of her cousin.

Hymns

(Dunstan's hymns are collected in *Sylvia G. Dunstan, In Search of Hope and Grace: 40 Hymns and Gospel Songs,* Chicago: GIA Publications, 1991, and Sylvia G. Dunstan, *Where the Promise Shines: 17 New Hymns,* Chicago: GIA Publications, 1995. The psalms are not published.)

All who hunger, gather gladly

Before you now, O God
Blest are the Innocents, Bethlehem's own
Blest be the God of Israel
Bless now, O God, the journey
Build your city on the hill
By birth, your creatures, cast from Eden's garden

Christ is born!
Christ is King! Let earthly powers
Christ is the Savior, the Lord once crucified
Christ, your love is overwhelming
Come gladly, come gaily, come gather together!

WITH TONGUES OF FIRE

Come, O holy house and worship!
Come to me, O weary traveler
Crashing waters at creation

Down Galilee's slow roadways

Eternal intercessor

For freedom Christ has set us free!
For the faithful who have answered
From the river to the desert
From wilderness a voice cries out

Go to the world!

How deep the silence of the soul

I believe in God almighty
In all our grief
In the beginning

Let angels and archangels
Lift up your hearts, believers!
Like a whisper in the heart
Lord, you lead through sea and desert

Now, O Lord, dismiss your servants

O come to Christ
O laughing light
O mystery profound
O saints, in splendour sing
One day in all time

Prisoners of your liberation

Send, O God, your Holy Spirit
Servants of the Savior
Shadows gather, deep and cold

SYLVIA DUNSTAN

Show me your hands, your feet, your side
Tell me again how hearts are lifted up
The storm is strong
The tomb is empty!
This holy covenant was made
This is your coronation
Those hearts that we have treasured
Through the heart of every city
Transform us

We gather in worship
We stand amazed before your love
When a star is shining over the eastern hills
When the Lord redeems the very least
When you, Lord, walked through Sabbath fields
Who is this who walks among us?

You, Lord, are both Lamb and shepherd
You walk along our shoreline

Metrical Psalms

27	My light and my salvation
28	Defender Lord, our anguished hearts
29	Ascribe to the Lord, O warriors of might
30	I will exalt the God who lifted me
31	In you we have taken refuge
31:9–16	Be merciful to me, O Lord
32	How blest are you whose sin
33	Sing to the Lord, you saints, sing loud and long
34	O bless and praise and glorify!
39	We keep watch on our ways
46	God's holy city we shall seek
47	All peoples, clap your hands and shout
50	The mighty one, our holy God
54	Save us, O God, by your name
55	Do not ignore my cry, O God
56	Be merciful to me, O God
57	In the shadow of your wings
58	You rulers, do you tell the truth?
59	O deliver, help and save!
60	You have rejected us, O God
61	O listen, God, our prayer we cry
62	Our life finds peace in God alone
63:1–9	O holy one, you are my God
66	Come now, and say what God has done
67	God of mercy and of blessings
72	Give justice as our ruler, God
80	Come, Israel's shepherd, high enthroned
85	You forgive your people, Lord
88	By day and night we cry to you
89	I will sing your love forever
90	Lord, you have been our dwelling place
91:9–16	If only we will make
92	Each morning we proclaim your love
93	You reign! And robed with majesty
94	Rise up, O judge of the earth
95	Come, sing in joy to God
98	Because you have done wonders
101	We sing your justice and your love

102	Hear my prayer and help me
103:1–13	My heart and my soul sing in praise to your name
104	Majesty and splendour
105:1–11	Give thanks to the Lord, our high holy one!
108	Our hearts are constant, O our God
111	We will extol you, Lord, with all our hearts
116	Even when we are afflicted
118	God's love endures forevermore
122	How glad I was to hear them say
126	When God restored the captives back to Zion
127	Do the builders work in vain?
130	Out of the depths, O God, we cry to you
133	With unity we live
137	By the Babylonian rivers
141	Like incense let my prayer rise up
147	Great is the God of power and might

Interview

[Since Sylvia Dunstan cannot be interviewed, we reprint here her Preface to *In Search of Hope and Grace: 40 Hymns and Gospel Songs* (Chicago: GIA, 1991).]

My grandparents taught me to sing. We sang around the piano, around the campfire, in the car, in the choir, wherever, whenever. Mostly we sang hymns, choruses, and gospel songs—these were to be the foundation of my religious understanding. I grew up unable to imagine life without singing. Grandmother entrusted my formal musical education to Sister St. Gregory at St. Joseph's convent. This was my first contact with Catholicism, since our family tended to the evangelical side of the United Church of Canada.

In the early seventies our church youth choir at St. James, Simcoe, relied heavily on the music of Ray Repp, the Medical Mission Sisters, and the religious use of secular pop music. The congregation was very tolerant as the youth choir inflicted various attempts at relevance upon them. We were young and energetic and sure that whatever moved us must surely move everyone. I began "writing songs" once I learned to play guitar. Most of these are now under a well-deserved and merciful curtain of oblivion.

WITH TONGUES OF FIRE

In 1974 I met Sister Miriam Therese Winter who taught me how to write scripture songs. These lessons in a sung interpretation of the biblical text freed me from the morass of using my own feelings as the sole basis for songs. M. T.'s influence also led me to explore musical and liturgical traditions outside post-war liberal Protestantism. The guitar was still my main resource musically. Eventually realizing that my tunes were all much of a muchness, I decided to concentrate on texts. Congregational resistance to unfamiliar tunes led me to use the hymn book tunes as the vehicle for the texts.

In this process of using hymn book tunes I learned that structure (meter, rhyme, etc.) empowered the people's singing. Since worship is intended to be the people's work, the hymn/song choices are best when they help the whole gathered people to pray and praise. I came to believe that "meaningful thoughts" in sloppy form are an impediment to the people's prayer, causing undue focus on the work itself, rather than pointing to the worship of God. This transition from guitar-strumming, meter-mangling self-indulgence to form-following, tradition-loving classicism took place from 1981 to 1983, during which I wrote almost nothing, but read and sang through hymn books untold. In January 1984 I wrote "Christus Paradox," which I showed to Alan Barthel. Over the past seven years, his encouragement and gentle bullying have been an impetus behind many of these hymns. Alan has also expanded my musical understanding, introducing me to a wide spectrum of resources, teaching me to work congenially with church musicians (another of those things I didn't learn in seminary).

May the God who heard the morning stars sing together hear us join in the song of all creation, ever eternal and new in our hearts.

Sylvia G. Dunstan

Toronto

SYLVIA DUNSTAN

For the faithful who have answered
　　when they heard your call to serve,
for the many ways you led them
　　testing will and stretching nerve,
for their work and for their witness
　　as they strove against the odds,
for their courage and obedience
　　we give thanks and praise, O God.

Many eyes have glimpsed the promise,
　　many hearts have yearned to see.
Many ears have heard you calling
　　us to greater liberty.
Some have fallen in the struggle.
　　Others still are fighting on.
You are not ashamed to own us.
　　We give thanks and praise, O God.

For this cloud of faithful witness,
　　for the common life we share,
for the work of peace and justice,
　　for the gospel that we bear,
for the vision that our homeland
　　is your love—deep, high and broad—
for the different roads we travel
　　we give thanks and praise, O God.

CHAPTER 5

Martin Franzmann

Thy strong word did cleave the darkness;
    At thy speaking it was done.
For created light we thank thee,
    While thine ordered seasons run.
Alleluia, alleluia!
    Praise to thee who light dost send!
Alleluia, alleluia!
    Alleluia without end!

Lo, on those who dwelt in darkness,
    Dark as night and deep as breath,
Broke the light of thy salvation,
    Breathed thine own life-giving breath.
Alleluia, alleluia!
    Praise to thee who light dost send!
Alleluia, alleluia!
    Alleluia without end!

Thy strong Word bespeaks us righteous;
    Bright as thine own holiness,
Glorious now, we press toward glory,
    And our lives our hopes confess.
Alleluia, alleluia!
    Praise to thee who light dost send!
Alleluia, alleluia!
    Alleluia without end!

From the cross thy wisdom shining
    Breaketh forth in conquering might;
From the cross forever beameth
    All thy bright redeeming light.
Alleluia, alleluia!
    Praise to thee who light dost send!
Alleluia, alleluia!
    Alleluia without end!

Give us lips to sing thy glory,
   Tongues thy mercy to proclaim,
Throats that shout the hope that fills us,
   Mouths to speak thy holy name.
Alleluia, alleluia!
   May the light which thou dost send
Fill our songs with alleluias,
   Alleluias without end!

God the Father, light-creator,
   To thee laud and honor be.
To thee, Light of Light begotten,
   Praise be sung eternally.
Holy Spirit, light-revealer,
   Glory, glory be to thee.
Mortals, angels, now and ever
   Praise the holy Trinity!

Biographical Sketch

Martin Franzmann (1907–76) was born on January 29, 1907, in Lake City, Minnesota, where his father, William Franzmann, was a Lutheran pastor. He was the third child in a family of nine children (five brothers and three sisters). His father was born in Westphalia, Germany. His mother, Else Emma Wilhelmine Griebling, came from Milwaukee, though her father had also been born in Germany. She loved hymns, and she sang them to her children along with all sorts of other musical snippets and games.

A voracious reader already as a child, by the time he went to Northwestern Preparatory School in Milwaukee it was clear he was a very talented person. He learned to play the cello, picked up enough piano to play chords for hymn tunes and folksong melodies, and wrote poetry. At school, when he was helping to get the auditorium ready for concerts, "he would make up a song with a story line which included everyone present and put it to a melody with a refrain that everyone could join in singing." When he came home from college his youngest brothers remember him challenging them to find a contradiction in a story he invented. "This resulted in some convoluted story lines that reached preposterous proportions." His vocabulary was immense, and when he needed a new word to express his thought, he coined it.

When Martin graduated from Northwestern, the College asked him to teach Greek and English. So he postponed going to seminary and from 1928 until 1930 served as an instructor at Northwestern. In 1930 he began studies at Wisconsin Lutheran Seminary in Thiensville, Wisconsin, but delayed completion there while he worked on a doctorate at the University of Chicago in 1931 and 1932. The University gave him the Daniel L. Shorey Traveling Fellowship, and in the spring of 1933 he spent three months in Greece.

He planned to return to the University of Chicago, but Pastor Arthur Katt at St. Peter's Church in Cleveland, Ohio, needed a teacher at the school there. He offered enough money to Franzmann and Alice Bentzin so that they could get married and come to St. Peter's in Cleveland where Alice had already been teaching. At St. Peter's Katt recognized Franzmann's gifts and encouraged him to translate and write hymns.

In 1935 Martin went back to seminary. He finished the Bachelor of Divinity degree in two rather than the normal three years and graduated in 1936. He was then asked to return to Northwestern College in Watertown, Wisconsin, as Professor of Classics, now a permanent rather than a temporary position. He served in that position, teaching English literature as well, until 1946. His two sons were born during this period.

In 1946 he was called to Concordia Seminary in St. Louis, Missouri, to teach New Testament. He stayed until 1969. His daughter was born there, he served on numerous committees at the Seminary and throughout the church and world, he published books and articles, and he wrote hymns. (He also got his driver's license—in 1962. Until then his wife Alice always drove.) He received an honorary doctorate from Springfield Seminary in 1956. In the 1940s and 1950s he continued the work he had begun on his Ph.D. at the University of Chicago, but he never finished it. The topic he was working on was "Legal Image and Legal Language in Greek Tragedy."

In 1969 Franzmann was offered a position at Westfield House in Cambridge, the Lutheran seminary of the Evangelical Lutheran Church in England. An Anglophile with an affinity for John Donne and George Herbert, he accepted the position, was also ordained (he had not been ordained earlier), and closed out his career there. In 1972 he retired to Wells in Somerset in the southwest of England and died in 1976.

Publications

Thy Strong Word: The Enduring Legacy of Martin Franzmann by Richard Brinkley. St. Louis: Concordia Publishing House, 1993.

Ha! Ha! Among the Trumpets. St. Louis: Concordia Publishing House, 1966.

"The Royal Banners Forward Go: Matthew 21:28–43; 22:1–14," *Concordia Theological Monthly* 32:3 (March 1961), pp. 157–61.

Come to the Feast: The Original and Translated Hymns of Martin H. Franzmann by Robin Leaver. St. Louis: Morning Star, 1994.

Hymns

Christ, our Lord, arose (trans.)

In Adam we have all been one
Isaiah in a vision did of old (trans.)

Jesus only, naught but Jesus (trans.)

Lord Jesus Christ in hidden ways
Lord, we will remember thee

O fearful place where he who knows our heart
O first and greatest of all servants
O God, O Lord of heaven and earth
O kingly love, that faithfully
O Lord, we praise thee (trans.)
O Thou who hast of thy pure grace
O Thou, who on th' accursed ground
O Thou, whose fiery blessing
Our Lord has laid his benison

Our Paschal Lamb, that sets us free

Praise thou the Lord, my soul (trans.)
Preach you the Word and plant it home

Rise again, ye lion-hearted (trans.)

The dawn has driven dark night away (trans.)
Though wisdom all her skills combine
Thou whose glory none can see
Thy strong word did cleave the darkness
Thy Word has been our daily bread
To songs of joy awaken thee (trans.)

Weary of all trumpeting
With high delight (trans.)

You spoke the word of truth

Interview

(Since Martin Franzmann cannot be interviewed, we reprint here his Reformation sermon, "Theology Must Sing" from Martin H. Franzmann, *Ha! Ha! Among the Trumpets* (St. Louis: Concordia, 1966), pp. 92–97. Franzmann wrote this (and his hymns as well) before concerns for inclusive language were being raised. It seems best to respect the historicity of the text, so it is given here as he wrote it.)

Let the Word of Christ dwell in you richly in all wisdom, teaching and admonishing one another in psalms and hymns and spiritual songs, singing with grace in your hearts to the Lord. Colossians 3:16

Theology is doxology. Theology must sing.

The church with psalms must shout,
No door can keep them out.

So at the Reformation, when the Word of Christ dwelt richly in men's hearts once more, when the peace of God was allowed to rule in men once more, there followed a burst of song almost without parallel in the history of the church. Here, too, the Reformation was not a revolution. It gave up nothing of the ancient song of the church that was good and profitable, and the Church of the Reformation ever since, when it has been true to its origin, has always welcomed each good new song.

But the history of the church's hymnody shows that the church has not always been true to its origin. The history of the church song is not an uninterrupted progress of triumph. So each generation of the church must try to test itself anew to see whether its song is true, to see whether its doxology is theology. St. Paul tells us that we are to teach and admonish one another with *spiritual* songs. If we can determine what "spiritual" means, we shall have the means of testing our song to see whether it be true.

"Spiritual" means wrought by the Holy Spirit, moved by Him, inspired by Him, coming from Him. The Holy Spirit is, first of all, a *holy* Spirit and speaks therefore with accents of His own, accents characteristic of Him and distinct from the world's. This does not mean that spiritual song does not use the words of men or sing the melodies of men. It does, but with a difference, just as the language of the New Testament speaks the common language of the common man and yet is no common speech. And so the church's song must speak with accents of its own, both in music and in text.

The Holy Spirit is the Firstfruits, the Earnest Money, the Seal of our heavenly inheritance. He is the Beginning and the Guarantee of heaven for us. A spiritual song must therefore breathe the air of eternity, must have a scent of heaven about it. It must be the prelude and the beginning of that new song which the church triumphant shall one day sing in the New Jerusalem.

The Holy Spirit is the confessor Spirit. "No man can say that Jesus is the Lord but by the Holy Ghost." If our songs are to be spiritual, they must confess; they must speak of the hope that is in us; they must tell of the mighty deeds of God in Christ in our behalf. Doxology, we say again, must be doctrinal: it must be theology.

The Holy Spirit is not a Spirit of slavery that slinks and cringes in fear. He is a Spirit of adoption and of sonship. Where this Spirit is, there is the free, confident atmosphere that exists between Father and child. Our songs must breathe that confidence, that sonship.

Where the Holy Spirit is, there is life, peace, and joy. There is life; we want no sluggish songs that crawl upon their belly and eat the dust. This peace is not a flat monotony of doing nothing, but the vibrant peace of a life of continual repentance, of continual renewal. And there is joy, that deep joy which is felt as the continued pulse of the church's life even in its most solemn moments of confession, humiliation, and prayer.

The Holy Spirit is a teaching Spirit, a Spirit that leads us into all truth. He is at the same time the Spirit that brings oneness and communion. Where this spirit works, there can be no such thing as a rampant self-asserting individualism, nor can there be a sentimental self-contemplating individualism. Where this Spirit is, there brethren know and feel themselves members one of another. They teach and admonish one another.

This Spirit is the Spirit of power. Our songs must soar:

> *The heavens are not too high,*
> *His praise may thither fly.*

The Spirit is at the same time the Spirit of love that condescends and suffers all things.

> *The ground is not too low,*
> *His praises there may grow.*

And He is the Spirit of a sound mind, so that we do not misuse the liberty which is wherever the Spirit is but welcome and exercise discipline, since we know by this Spirit's teaching that "God is not the Author of confusion but of peace."

As we survey the hymnody of the Reformation we can but gratefully acknowledge that God has here given the church a song that is really spiritual. And as we survey all hymnody we must acknowledge that the Holy Spirit worked not only in the Reformation but in all times and in all places in the one Christian and apostolic church, that in the best of what Christian poets and Christian music makers have produced the church possesses so vast a store of the absolutely excellent that it need never stoop to substitutes.

And yet there has always been a terrible fascination in *Ersatz,* especially for a sick church, a church grown so languid that it cannot bear to live in the tension of the last days. And so we have, instead of the splendid picture of the church universal making a full-throated, joyful noise unto the Lord, the picture of the weary church sitting in a padded pew, weeping softly and elegantly into a lace handkerchief.

And the amazing thing is how eloquent men can grow in defense of this shoddy *Ersatz* hymnody. They begin by criticizing the good hymns as "hard to sing." One might ask in return, Why must a hymn be easy? Who has ever said that it should be easy? Look at the woodcut of Albrecht Dürer's where he depicts that scene from the Apocalypse in which those that came from the great tribulation, who have washed their robes in the blood of the Lamb, sing their heavenly song. Look at those faces, their intensity of concentration, faces almost contorted with the energy of their devotion, if you would know what singing with grace in your hearts to the Lord really means.

The fact that there is an amazing agreement on the part of hymnodists and musicians in all parts of the church as to what constitutes a good hymn counts for little with these critics. The hymnodists' passion for perfection is viewed with suspicion, as a sort of professional snobbery, and is usually countered with, "I don't know much about it, but I know what I like." That is really the ultimate in snobbery. To pit my piping, squeaking, little ego against all the good gifts that God has given His church! It is worse than snobbery; it is ingratitude. It is as though God had led us out into His great, wide world and shown us ripe, waving fields of grain and said to us, "Here is bread, and all for you." It is as though God had shown us all the cattle on a thousand hills and said to us, "Here is milk and cheese and butter and meat for you" and we then replied: "No thanks! It is not to my taste. I'd rather go to a messy, dusty, fly-infested county fair and eat cotton candy."

Another argument might be called the "tin whistle" argument. Its essence is something like this: "After all, a man can make music on a tin whistle to the glory of God, and God will be pleased to hear it." True, true, true—if God has given him nothing but a tin whistle; but God has given us so infinitely much more. When He has given us all the instruments under heaven with which to sing His praises, then the tin whistle is no longer humility but a perverse sort of pride.

Perhaps the most insidious attack of all is the one that says: "Yes, these hymns are inferior, but we must use them as stepping-stones to something better. We must use them to train up the people for the solid food of our best hymnody." I am reminded here of a little poem on an artist who sold himself out, a poem that is not nearly as funny as it sounds:

He found a formula for drawing comic rabbits,
And the formula for drawing comic rabbits paid,
But in the end he could not change the habits
That the formula for drawing comic rabbits made.

We had better be careful about indulging in such condescensions, lest we too find the comic rabbits too powerful for us.

Rather let the Word of Christ dwell in us richly, and then we shall inevitably find, sing, and produce the best in song. We must produce. The song of the church must be an unending song. The church must cherish the best, but its song should not be a mere repetition of the song in the past. Then shall we sing with grace, with all the emphasis on God and a most unsentimental subordination of ourselves. We shall sing to the Lord. With our song we shall guide one another continually to the center and foundation of the Christian's life and thus really teach and admonish one another. We shall sing in our hearts; the whole man will sing. We shall see then realized the ideal of all Christian song: the whole man with all his powers, with all the skills and gifts that God has bestowed upon him wholly bent on giving utterance to the peace that rules within him, wholly given to the purpose of letting the Word of Christ that dwells in him richly become articulate and audible through him to the upbuilding of the church and the glory of God. Then shall our theology be doxology. Then shall we sing with Mary: "My soul doth magnify the Lord, and my spirit hath rejoiced in God, my Savior...for He that is mighty hath done to me great things, and holy is His name." Amen

Weary of all trumpeting, weary of all killing,
Weary of all songs that sing promise, non-fulfilling
We would raise, O Christ, one song;
We would join in singing that great music
 pure and strong,
Wherewith heaven is ringing.

Captain Christ, O lowly Lord, Servant King, Your dying

WITH TONGUES OF FIRE

Bade us sheathe the foolish sword, bade us
    cease denying.
Trumpet with your Spirit's breath through ·
    each height and hollow;
Into your self-giving death, call us all to follow.

To the triumph of your cross summon all the living;
Summon us to love by loss, gaining all in giving,
Suffering all, that we may see triumph in surrender;
Leaving all, that we may be partners in your splendor.

CHAPTER 6

Fred Pratt Green

When in our music God is glorified
    And adoration leaves no room for pride,
It is as though the whole creation cried:
    Alleluia, alleluia, alleluia!

How oft, in making music, we have found
    A new dimension in the world of sound
As worship moved us to a more profound
    Alleluia, alleluia, alleluia!

So has the Church, in liturgy and song,
    In faith and love, through centuries of wrong,
Borne witness to the truth in every tongue:
    Alleluia, alleluia, alleluia!

And did not Jesus sing a psalm that night
    When utmost evil strove against the light?
Then let us sing for whom he won the fight:
    Alleluia, alleluia, alleluia!

Let every instrument be tuned for praise;
    Let all rejoice who have a voice to raise;
And may God give us faith to sing always:
    Alleluia, alleluia, alleluia!

Biographical Sketch

Frederick Pratt Green was born in 1903 in Roby, now a suburb of Liverpool, England, to Charles and Hannah (Greenwood) Green. Charles ran a leather manufacturing business and was a Wesleyan Methodist and Local Preacher. Hannah was an Anglican. As a child Fred worshiped at Childwall Parish (Anglican) Church and later at Claremount Road Wesleyan Church (Wallasey). He attended Huyton

High School, Wallasey Grammar School, Rydal School (a Methodist Public School), and Didsbury Theological College.

At first Pratt Green wanted to become an architect. Before Didsbury Theological College, however, he worked for four years with his father in the leather business. At Didsbury he developed yet another interest, writing, with a play called *Farley Goes Out*. In 1928, the year he left Didsbury, he wrote his first hymn, "God Lit a Flame in Bethlehem." The same year he became enamored of Marjorie Dowsett. His hymn writing was considerably postponed, but he and Marjorie Dowsett were married three years later and have been married now for more than 60 years.

Pratt Green was accepted for the Wesleyan Methodist Ministry in 1924, the year before he went to the Theological College. He served the following Circuits: Severn Valley, Filey (and as Chaplain of Hunmanby Hall School), Otley, Bradford (Manningham), Ilford (London), and Finsbury Park (London). He was Superintendent of the Dome Mission (Brighton), the South Norwood (London) Circuit, and the Sutton (London) Circuit, and Chairman of the York and Hull District. He retired to Norwich in 1969 when he began a new career as a hymn writer.

Pratt Green's poetic abilities were being developed before his hymn writing career began. After coming to the Finsbury Park Circuit in 1944, he paid a pastoral call to Fallon Webb, the father of one of his Sunday school children. Webb, in spite of his arthritis, had an intense interest in poetry. When he discovered that Pratt Green had written some poems, he suggested that they each write a poem and criticize the other's piece at their next encounter. They continued this practice until Webb's death 20 years later.

At his retirement in 1969, Fred had planned to spend time doing pastels. However, he accepted an invitation to serve on a committee which was to prepare a supplement to the *Methodist Hymn-Book* (eventually published as *Hymns and Songs*). The committee asked Fred to write hymns for topics where hymns seemed to be lacking, and hymn writing replaced water colors. John Wilson, Director of Music at Charterhouse from 1947 to 1965, a member of the committee and an astute hymnologist, was especially helpful to Fred's development, as was Erik Routley who learned of Fred's gifts and encouraged them.

By 1982 Fred Pratt Green was widely recognized for his hymn writing and came to the United States to receive an honorary doctorate in Humane Letters from Emory University. He served as Vice President of the Hymn Society of Great Britain and Ireland, Associate of the Royal School of Church Music, and was made a Fellow of the Hymn Society in the United States and Canada.

Fred now lives in retirement from his hymn writing. He says it is good to know when to stop! He remains a remarkable Christian gentleman who is an outstanding hymn writer of our time. (Some would call him the Charles Wesley of the 20th century. He rejects this, saying, "We are all dwarfs alongside Wesley and Watts!")

Works and Collections

The Hymns and Ballads of Fred Pratt Green. Carol Stream: Hope Publishing Company, 1982.

Later Hymns and Ballads and Fifty Poems. Carol Stream: Hope Publishing Company, 1989.

Hymns

(This list is taken from *Later Hymns and Ballads and Fifty Poems* [Carol Stream: Hope Publishing Company, 1989], pp. 198–205. The first lines of refrains are indicated by the italic.)

A church is *heaven's gate*
After darkness, light
After the Lamb had broken the Seventh Seal
A hundred years! How small a part
Alive, alive O!
All is ready for the Feast!
All my hope is firmly grounded
All of you share my gladness
All the sky is bright
All they wanted was a shelter
All who worship God in Jesus, all who serve the Son of Man
A man had been robbed of all he had
A new day bids us wake
A New Year confronts us: and must it be true

WITH TONGUES OF FIRE

Angelic hosts proclaimed him, when he came, when he came
An Upper Room did our Lord prepare
As athletes gather round the track
As darkness turns to light
As evening turns to night
As Jesus Christ lay fast asleep
As we Christians gather
A tree there grew in Eden's glade

Before the Legions marched away
Blest be the King whose coming is in the name of God!
Break forth, O pure celestial light
But here's a bouncing ball
By gracious powers so wonderfully sheltered
By the Cross which did to death our only Saviour

Christ has died!
Christ is preached in Caesarea
Christ is the world's Light, he and none other
Come, celebrate with us (another version of "Unite us, Lord, this
    day")
Come, let us all renew the vows
Come quickly, Lord, they prayed
Come, share our Easter joy
Come, share with us, as every Christian can
Come, share with us the joyful news
Come, sing a song of harvest
Come to us who wait here, and tarry not!

Daily we come, dear Master
Dark against an eastern sky
Dear Lord, from youth to age

Father, in weakness give us strength
Father of every race
For each kind of music that adds a dimension
For forty days we mourn the day
For the fruits of his (all) (this) creation

Forty years the Chosen People
For us all a child was born
Friends, we begin tomorrow

Glorious the day when Christ was born
God bless us all who at this time
God in his love for us lent us this planet
God is God and his the glory
God is good! How God has helped us
God is here! As we his (your) people
God is our Song, and every singer blest
God lit a flame in Bethlehem
God of the nations, God of all who live
'God rested on the Seventh Day'
God saw that it was good
God triumphs, for he is righteousness
Good neighbours, do not ask them why
Great our joy as now we gather

Have mercy, Lord
He healed the darkness of my mind
Here are the bread and wine
Here is one whose eager mind
Here, Master, in this quiet place
Here's a donkey you may trust
Here, where past generations
He was homeless when he came
He who died comes to reign!
His the gracious invitation
Honour God's saints, however lowly
Hosanna! Come and see
How blest are they who trust in Christ
How can we sing our songs of faith
How clear is our vocation, Lord
How crowded the Pool of Bethesda
How dark was the night of his coming!
How good it is in praise and prayer
How good it is when we agree

How great a mystery
How great our debt to pioneers, who in our nation's youth
How great the debt we owe
How hard it was for them to stay
How long, the prophets cried, how long
How many are the saints of God
How many evils spoil our lives
How many saints our God has given
How privileged we are
How rich at Eastertide
How rich is God's creation
How right it is to celebrate
How right that we should offer
How sacred is this place!
How shall we thank the God of grace
How short a time our church's years
How wonderful this world of Thine (God's)
Hurry, hurry, brothers; do not more delay

Infant in the stall, all our sins destroy!
In that land which we call Holy
It is God who holds the nations in the hollow of his hand
It may be that they were Magi
It shocked them that the Master did not fast
It was fair weather when we set sail
It was Jesus who said we must persevere

Jesus Christ, for forty days
Jesus, how strong is our desire
Jesus, I know you came
Jesus in the olive grove
Jesus is God's gift to us
Jesus is the Lord of Glory
Jesus, Redeemer, friend of the friendless

Lest we forget, let young and old
Let every Christian pray
Let my vision, Lord, be keen and clear this day

Let us all praise him
Let us gaze today upon her
Let us praise Creation's Lord
Let us rejoice in Christ
Let us welcome each other, we people who gather
Life has many rhythms, every heart its beat
Life has no mystery as great
Listen to what the handbells say
Little children, welcome!
Lo! God's Son is now ascended
Long ago, prophets knew
Look, the sun awakes the sky
Lord and Master
Lord, as worship starts
Lord, do you trust yourself to me?
Lord God, in whom all worlds
Lord God, when we complain
Lord, I know your Word will lead me
Lord in an hour of bleak despair
Lord, in our lonely hours
Lord, in your timeless Kingdom
Lord, I repent my sin
Lord Jesus, once a child
Lord Jesus, you were homeless
Lord, let us listen when you speak!
Lord, now it's time to pray
Lord of every art and science
Lord, we believe for us you lived and died
Lord, we come to ask your blessing
Lord, we have come at your own invitation
Lord, when we find it hard to pray
Lord, when you came to seek the lost
Lord, when you gave your Church-to-be
Lord, when you singled out the Three
Lord, you are at many tables
Lord, you do not need our praises
Lo! Today into our world the Word is born
Love is the name he bears

Loving Lord, as now we gather

Man cannot live on bread alone
Mary looks upon her child
Mary sang to her Son: 'Don't you cry, little one!'
Men go to Galilee when they are in despair

Never shall we forget
Never was a day so bright
Nicodemus comes by night
Now, as we keep this famous fast
Now David was a shepherd boy
Now God be praised, the work is done!
Now it is evening
Now, let us all, in hymns of praise
Now praise the hidden God of Love
Now shall the Church, this day of celebration
Now Simeon was an agéd man
Now that harvest crops are gathered
Now the silence, Lord, is broken

O Child, most truly God's own Son
O Christ, the Healer, we have come
Of all the Spirit's gifts to me
Of the many who flocked to hear you
O God of all, our Servant God
O Jesus Christ, as you awake
Once upon a time they went
On each Thanksgiving Day
One day we shall have good news
One God and Father of us all!
One in Christ, we meet together
One morning on that misty shore
One woman none could heal
On the road to Damascus, he's blinded by light
O round as the world is the orange you give us!
Other gospel there is none
O tidings of comfort and joy

FRED PRATT GREEN

Our fathers lived by faith
Out of our world, out of its distress

Praise God, transcendent in glory
Praise her, as Jesus did!
Praise the God of our salvation
Praise the God whose world this is
Praise the Lord for all delights (compulsory revision)
Praise the Lord for all pioneers
Pray for our cities! Grown too fast
Pray for the Church, afflicted and oppressed
Prepare us, Lord, in quietness of mind

Rejoice in God's saints (this day of all days)
Rejoice in God's saints, today and all days
Rejoice that he who came that night redeems us all
Rejoice with heart and voice
Rejoice with us in God, the Trinity
Repent the follies, faults, and sins
Rest in peace, earth's journey ended
Ring, bells, ring, ring, ring!
Ring the bells of Bethlehem
Ring the bells of every town

Salvation! There's no better word
Say you this pagan mistletoe
Seek the Lord who now is present
Seven times Christ spoke upon that hill of death
She stood, her guilt laid bare
She went alone to Jacob's Well
Sing, one and all, a song of celebration
Sing praises, one and all
Sing to the Lord a new song, for he does wonders
Sing, you who are the family of God
Sleep, my little King of kings
Some offer God their busy hands
Soon may we see your will done on earth, Lord
So toss, toss, toss the golden pancake

Summer is over; the dark fields lie fallow
Sun of Righteousness, arise

Take me as your disciple, Lord
The calf said moo!
The Church, in Advent, from of old
The Church of Christ in every age
The door is open, the table spread
The first day of the week
The fountain of joy is in Heaven
The God who sent the prophets (compulsory revision)
The grace of life is theirs
The newly-born, they are not always welcome
The night is nearly over
Then let us bind ourselves this day
There are songs for us all to sing
There is a love that reaches out to all
There's joy in remembrance this notable day
'There's no room in the ark for donkeys,' said Shem
There's snow on the mountain and ice on the pond
The Word is born this very night
The world's great age is yet to be
They built a school on Bowthorpe Hill
This carol we will gladly sing
This day may God inspire us
This heart of mine is in deep anguish
      (not for further reproduction)
This is the gospel we hold fast
This is the night of his coming to earth
This is the threefold truth
This joyful Eastertide
Though I speak with tongues of men and angels
Though Love is the greatest of the three
Three years they had known him as Master and Lord
Thus Angels sung, and thus sing we
Today how sacred is this place
To mock your reign, O dearest Lord
Turo, luro, luro, who can measure

FRED PRATT GREEN

Two brothers came to blows

Unite us, Lord, this day (later version of "Come, celebrate with us")

We come to worship you, O Lord, whose glory is so great
We enter, Lord, and are at home
We haven't come from far
We honour, one in Christ, this day
We look into your heavens and see
We were born in Glasgow City, as everyone should know
We weren't dressed up in our sabbath best
We who worship bear our witness
We will serve the Lord with joy in the Church and in the world
We will sing you a song
We would ask, Lord, for your Spirit!
We would rejoice again, and yet again
What Adam's disobedience cost
What a joy it is to sing
What are they: freedom fighters, common thieves
What does he ask of us, our Saviour Christ
What have you done to die in anguish
What is our earth but a prison
What joy it is to worship here
What shall our greeting be
What shepherds saw, by stable light
What's in a name? No more or less
What sort of man did Pilate see
What tale is this our women bring?
What the Spirit says to the Churches
When Father Abraham went out
When God created herbs
When humans grew up on our planet
When, in our music, God is glorified
When Jesus came preaching the Kingdom of God
When Jesus came to Jordan
When Jesus walked by Galilee
When loaves are on the table
When our confidence is shaken

When ringers in full circle stand
When the Church of Jesus
When Wesley came to Bristol Town
Where Christ is, his Church is there
Where does our salvation start?
Where shall we lay him
Where Temple offerings are made
Who comes riding on a donkey's back?
Who is it whistling on the hill
Who is running up the street
Whom shall I send? our Maker cries
Who was first to strike a spark?
Winter's here, with falling snow
With all fellow Christians who gather tonight
Wonderful the world of Nature

You are Christ's feet here today in the world
You dear Lord, resplendent within our darkness, grant us your light
'You must be ready', the Master said
Yours be the glory, yours, O Risen Friend!
Your voice, my God, calls me by name

Zacchaeus in the pay of Rome

Interview

PW: Could you give some sense of your theological accents?

FPG: I am typical of Methodist ministers in being "middle of the way," concerned rather with the practical application and expression of our faith than with theological controversy. That means I am neither an extreme modernist nor a fundamentalist. My own personal accent would be on the cross of Christ as both demonstration and expression of the redemptive power of love. This I believe to be the essential and unique message of the religion of Jesus to the world.

PW: Are there any hymns that you wished you had written?

FPG: This question intrigues me! As nearly all my hymn writing has been in response to requests or commissions, I am more surprised by what I *have* written than worried about what I *have not* written!

PW: *What do you wish you had not written?*

FPG: Sometimes when I have to sing my own hymns, I regret a word of careless expression and think of something better. Only two hymns cause me some embarrassment.

First, in "Christ Is the World's Light," the phrase "he and none other" is, of course, theologically sound, but it savors of the religiously arrogant. What about the Buddha who is to millions of sincere believers the "light of the world"? I have an uncomfortable feeling that in the modern world, when the real teaching of the Buddha is better understood, a less imperialistic phrase would have been closer to the real truth: "Christ is the world's Light, for us none other."

Second, in the hymn "The God Who Sent the Prophets" which appeared in *Hymns and Psalms* (no. 454), I used the word *holocaust* in a general sense. Almost immediately after *Hymns and Psalms* was published, the famous film about the extermination of the Jews by the Nazis gave the word *holocaust* a new and infamous meaning. It makes my hymn seem to suggest that the Jews brought their extermination deservedly upon their own heads! Now I would urge that the last line read, "Reap judgment in the end." This is referred to in the *Companion to Hymns and Psalms.*

PW: *How do you see the hymn functioning in worship?*

FPG: Chiefly in three ways: to *inspire* a congregation to worship; to *instruct* a congregation in Christian truth and practice; and to *help unite* Christians of various denominations. I am also aware of the value of hymns in private devotion (private worship), as many letters to me have testified. Hymns have a pastoral influence in the life of the church.

PW: *How do you perceive your influence? Is it regional or broader?*

FPG: It still surprises me that my hymns are sung by almost all the Christian churches and groups, and that they have spread widely throughout the English-speaking world. A few have been translated into other languages.

PW: How do you see your work in relation to late 20th-century hymnody generally?

FPG: Hymnologists have decreed that the work of a group of us writing hymns in the late 1960s, 1970s, and 1980s amounted to an explosion after the dull period of the first half of the century. We have accepted the responsibility! We saw our work as meeting a need: to express the insights of our time in the language of today (now more accurately "yesterday"). We were specially conscious of the gaps in current hymnody, particularly in relation to social justice, racial equality, world peace, the protection of the environment, and similar issues. This need was felt by all the churches. It meant first of all a series of exploratory supplements to existing hymnals, followed by the inclusion of new hymns in the hymnals that followed. The new *English Hymnal* was almost alone in regarding us with extreme caution. The material we produced quickly appealed to American editors, and in due course all the American mainstream churches produced hymnals in which our work found a generous place. This movement may be said now to have produced a further detonation. There must be at least 20 hymn writers whose work is highly regarded and accepted both in Britain and America.

PW: What in the current scene gratifies you?

FPG: The liberation of hymnody in both range and expression. This kind of revolution is no new phenomenon. The revivalist hymnody and the preservation of the negro spiritual were liberating in their day and still enrich hymnody. That this process goes on is gratifying, especially in an age of change like ours.

PW: Are there any trends which alarm you?

FPG: "Alarm" is too strong a word. I view the repetitious kind of song which can excite a congregation without deepening understanding and affecting practice as unattractive—to me personally. But I have to confess that I prefer quiet worship and would make a better Quaker that a Pentecostalist.

PW: What do you think the future of American/English hymnody holds?

FPG: Much depends on whether Christianity continues to decline as a major influence on life in our western society. We are moving into a new world, technologically and psychologically. "The Spirit bloweth where it listeth." I am no prophet.

PW: *What do you regard as the three (or two or one) most representative hymns you have written?*

FPG: I find this question difficult to answer. Does it mean representative of my own work or of "the modern movement"? I will content myself by choosing three hymns which I happen to feel are "me" rather than popular.

1) "When in Our Music God Is Glorified," not so often sung in England, but popular in America. This hymn expresses my deep love of music, the greatest of the arts (!) and important in the worship of the church.

2) "For the Fruit of All Creation" because it expresses my strong belief that the gospel has social implications too often overlooked in a materialistic society.

3) "An Upper Room Did Our Lord Prepare" because in its quiet way it expresses a strong conviction, expresses what Holy Communion means to me, and for its personal association which I need not describe. I would like it sung as a solo at my funeral.

PW: *How do you feel you have been treated by hymnal editors?*

FPG: Almost invariably with courtesy and consideration, but this may partly be due to my method of presenting a new text, whether commissioned or not. I offer a first draft, inviting criticism and a willingness to accept it and profit by it, as long as it does not go contrary to some strong conviction. When a church commissions a work rather than an editor, this method is especially helpful because the hymn is not only mine, it is also theirs. More than once a very valuable suggestion has improved a hymn.

I have one complaint. Why do editors (music editors?) nearly always disregard the hymn writer's strong feeling about the appropriate tune? I almost invariably write to a particular tune. Sometimes I feel the choice of another tune weakens my text.

PW: *What or who influenced you to write hymns? Why do you do it?*

FPG: The first part of the question is easily answered: our great English hymnologists John Wilson and Erik Routley. They advised me over most of my earlier hymns, and I have had a long association with John Wilson of great benefit to myself. It is well-known, I think, that I began to write hymns simply because my church, through a committee to which I was elected, thought my experience as a poet would enable me to judge new material as to its suitability in a reputable hymnal. Almost immediately they said, "You call yourself a poet; go and write the hymns we need." I obeyed.

PW: *What process do you follow when writing a hymn?*

FPG: I work hard at the text and hope that that mysterious thing called inspiration will be granted me.

PW: *Is there anything you would like to add?*

FPG: Yes, I would mention that all the royalties from my hymns go to the Pratt Green Trust for the encouragement and study of hymnody.

> For the fruit of all creation,
>   thanks be to God.
> For his gifts to every nation,
>   thanks be to God.
> For the plowing, sowing, reaping,
> silent growth while we are sleeping,
> future needs in earth's safekeeping,
>   thanks be to God.
>
> In the just reward of labor,
>   God's will be done.
> In the help we give our neighbor,
>   God's will be done.
> In our worldwide task of caring
> for the hungry and despairing,
> in the harvests we are sharing,
>   God's will be done.
>
> For the harvest of the Spirit,
>   thanks be to God.

FRED PRATT GREEN

For the good we all inherit,
    thanks be to God.
For the wonders that astound us,
for'the truths that still confound us,
most of all that Love has found us,
    thanks be to God.

CHAPTER 7

Fred Kaan

For the healing of the nations,
    Lord, we pray with one accord;
for a just and equal sharing
    of the things that earth affords.
To a life of love in action
    help us rise and pledge our word.

Lead us, Father, into freedom,
    from despair your world release;
that redeemed from war and hatred,
    all may come and go in peace.
Show us how through care and goodness
    fear will die and hope increase.

All that kills abundant living,
    let it from the earth be banned;
pride of status, race or schooling,
    dogmas that obscure your plan.
In our common quest for justice
    may we hallow life's brief span.

You, creator-God, have written
    your great name on humankind;
for our growing in your likeness
    bring the life of Christ to mind;
that by our response and service
    earth its destiny may find.

Biographical Sketch

Fred Kaan was born in 1929 in Harlem, the Netherlands, to a nominally Christian family. After his Baptism, except for occasional Sunday school attendance, he did not go to church as a boy. His interest in theology was stimulated by high school religious education teachers, among them Hendrikus Berkhof who became Professor of Dogmatics and Biblical Theology at the University of Leiden and wrote, among other things, *Christ and the Powers.*

Kaan endured the Nazi occupation of Holland as a youth. His father was a member of the Dutch Resistance, his family hid a Jew and a political prisoner in their home, his mother almost starved to death, and three grandparents died of starvation.

Kaan's first inclination was to be a painter, but he began studying theology in 1949 at the State University of Utrecht. Correspondence with a pen pal in London and an article on congregationalism by Karl Barth led him to England, where in 1954 he graduated with a B.A. from Bristol University. His other degrees are an honorary Th.D. from Debrecen Theological Academy in Hungary in 1978, a Ph.D. from Geneva Theological College in 1984 where his dissertation was entitled "Emerging Language in Hymnody," and a London Certificate in Counseling in 1989.

Kaan was ordained in 1955 into the Congregational Union of England and Wales, a denomination which later merged with the Presbyterian Church of England and the Churches of Christ to become the United Reformed Church in the United Kingdom. He served Windsor Road Congregational Church in Barry, South Wales from 1955 to 1963, and The Pilgrim Church in Plymouth from 1963 to 1968 as pastor. Especially at the latter his hymn writing was stimulated. Not finding hymns they wanted, Kaan and the church prepared their own hymn supplement which they called *Pilgrim Praise.*

From the beginning of his ministry at South Wales, one of Kaan's hallmarks was the establishment of international contacts. His posts from 1968 to 1978 will come therefore as no surprise: Minister-Secretary of the International Congregational Council, London and Geneva; Secretary for the Department of Cooperation and Witness, World Alliance of Reformed Churches, Geneva, and concurrently: Editor of the four-language *Reformed Press Service,* Managing Editor of the quarterly journal *Reformed World,* and co-producer of the ecumenical radio program *Intervox.* Internationalism also characterized his family life: his wife was born in Indonesia, and his children hold dual nationality (Dutch/British). The elder son is married to a Swede, the younger to a Hungarian, while the daughter married an Englishman. Between them they have a command of nine different languages.

In 1978 Kaan returned to England to become Moderator of the West Midlands Province of the United Reformed Church in the United Kingdom. In 1985 he declined renomination to that post to oppose any "hierarchical thinking" and became team minister of the Central (ecumenical) Church, Swindon, and minister of Penhill United Reformed Church.

Throughout his life and in addition to his other responsibilities, Kaan has traveled extensively, has held numerous ecumenical positions, and has been a part of many ecumenical gatherings. Some of this has been related to hymnody. He was a member of the editorial working group for the ecumenical and international hymnal *Cantate Domino*. He has been an advisor on worship and has lectured on hymn writing. He is a member of the Hymn Society in the United States and Canada, the Hymn Society of Great Britain and Ireland, and the Internationale Arbeitsgemeinschaft für Hymnologie.

Hymn Collections

Pilgrim Praise. London: Stainer and Bell, 1972.

Break Not the Circle (American edition). Carol Stream: Hope Publishing Company, 1975.

Break Not the Circle (English edition). Leeds: John Paul, the Preacher's Press, 1983.

Hymns and Songs from Sweden. London: Stainer & Bell, 1976.

The Hymn Texts of Fred Kaan. London: Stainer & Bell; Carol Stream: Hope Publishing Company, 1985.

Planting Trees and Sowing Seeds. Oxford: Oxford University Press; Carol Stream: Hope Publishing Company, 1989.

Hymns

A house has different rooms
All that Christians have in life
Almond trees, renewed in bloom

Although our Lord has left us
Although we go our separate ways
As the glory of creation
As the vine is to the branches
As we break the bread

Before all time, love's logic spoke the Word
Before a Word was said
Bless and keep us, Lord
Bread and wine for two or three
Bread, feeding people's hope
Break not the circle
By each other sentenced

Choose life, choose love
Christian people, serve the Lord
Christ is alive!
Christ is coming, Christ has come
Christ is crucified today
Christ is risen, Christ is living
City of man, how rich and right
Come among us, loving Spirit
Come and be surprised, all nations
Come, dare to be all that you are in Christ
Come, O Holy Spirit
Committed to Christ

Divided by cultures, traditions and speech
Down to earth, as a dove

Each morning with its newborn light
Each Sunday brings to mind again
Each year we sing with bated Christmas voice
Earth is shaken to its bed-rock
Establish, Lord, your kingdom

Faith, while trees are still in blossom
Father, help your people

FRED KAAN

Father, we long to be people more human
Father, who in Jesus found us
For all who have enriched our lives
For ourselves no longer living
For the crowd of thousands
For the healing of the nations
For this day of new beginnings
Freedom is to people

Gathered here from many nations
Give thanks to God for Word of Christmas
Glory and anguish to God in the height
Glory to God in the highest
God among us, Sense of life
God, as with silent hearts we bring to mind
God calls his people firm to stand
God calls us to the fellowship of living
God gave us in trust to hold
God is unique and one
God makes his rain to fall
God of Adam, God of Joseph
God of Bible and tradition
God of Eve and God of Mary
God's kingdom is among us
God's word throughout the ages
God the narrator
God! When human bonds are broken
God who spoke in the beginning
God will, when he comes down to earth

Help us accept each other
He's back in the land of the living
How can creation's voice be still
How many fruits we gain
How wide is life for living

I can on God implicitly rely
If you have ears, then listen

WITH TONGUES OF FIRE

I look for the city
In the beginning: God!
I throw my rejoicing
'It's Jesus we want'

Jesus, shepherd of our souls

Let all who share one bread
Let Christian people practice praise and love
Let us our hearts and voices raise
Let us talents and tongues employ
Life could be good and rich and whole
Like fields awaiting the sowing of seed
Lord, as we rise
Lord, confronted with your might
Lord, do not hold yourself apart
Lord God, we seek your face
Lord God, who on the Friday of creation
Lord, how majestic is your name
Lord of the living
Lord, while the world with war and hatred burns
Lord, you made the world
Love has come among us!

Mary, Mary, quite contrary
Modern people have cities for their home
Move me to crying
My longing is older than light years of sun

Now in the name of him
Now join we, to praise the creator
Now let us from this table rise
Now let us translate

O God who gave humanity its name
O God of the eternal now
O Holy Spirit, hear us as we pray
Our faults divide and hinder

FRED KAAN

Our God has given his Son to the earth
Out of deep, unordered water
Out of our failure to create
Out of our night of day

Peace be with all who worship here
Praise the Lord with faithful cry
Put peace into each other's hands

"Qui cantat, bis orat"

Raising our hands as a sign of rejoicing

See how swarming birds of heaven
Seek your rest in the storm winds
Sing high to God who once upon a time
Sing we a song of high revolt
Sing we of the modern city
Son of the Father
Surrounded by a world of need

Thank you, God, that long before all time
Thank you, O lord, for the time that is now
The church is like a table
The day will come
The earth, the sky, the oceans
The fullness of the earth is God's alone
The great commandment of our Lord
The language of the Hebrews
The love of God is broad
The trouble with many of our churches
The wall is down
They saw you as the local builder's son
The whole earth is fulfilled
They set out on their homeward road
This is the day
Time is full to overflowing
Today I live

Tomorrow Christ is coming
To live at peace with others
To love our sisters, brothers
To show by touch and word

Upstairs? Downstairs? God is there!

Wealthy man, you are imprisoned
We come uneasy, Lord
We come with empty hands, intent on sharing
We dare not, Father, ask to be as one
We have a king who rides a donkey
We long to learn to praise
We meet you, O Christ
We need to breathe, for living
We pause to give thanks
We praise your name
We rise to respond
We tingle with excitement
We turn to you
We utter our cry
We who bear the human name
Welcome, day of the Lord!
Were the world to end tomorrow
When any person is to Christ united
When in his own image
When Jesus sat down
When Noah's ark was high and dry
When, O God, our faith is tested
Wherever we may go
While still the world is full of people
With fervent dedication
With grateful hearts

You are on earth, Lord Jesus Christ
You call and create
You called me, Father, by my name
You gave us, God, this earth to hold and cherish

You lead us, Lord
You, Lord, who chose to care
You who by burdens hard oppressed
You who through the city

Interview

PW: *Could you give some sense of your theological accents?*

FK: May I refer you to my introductory article in *The Hymn Texts of Fred Kaan?*

(Author's note: One might summarize that introduction by saying Kaan argues for singing a *new* song to the Lord, "a new hymn for a new day." He quotes Albert van den Heuvel with fervor. Van den Heuvel finds it "nonsense" that we learn of "a new corporate existence in community" but "continue to emphasize the individualism of the 18th and 19th centuries," or "speak of the secular city and sing of our "heavenly home," or "work for an urban faith and ... sing on Sunday about nothing but nature." He points out that it is "either comic or tragic to hear a congregation which speaks of its service and witness in the modern world sing about an ingrown concentration on their own salvation."

Kaan is frustrated and angry about "remote symbolism, the antiquated terminology, and the socially unacceptable nature of much that was on offer" in our hymnody and wants to press for "the *immanence of God* and the *real presence of Christ* in accessible, honestly contemporary English." The first hymn texts he wrote therefore were Communion and Post-Communion pieces that probed the connection from the Table to the world.

Kaan argues that the world needs to write the agenda and that Christ is in our midst. He wants to balance what he sees as the interminable weight we have laid on Jesus as God, by emphasizing Jesus as a human being alongside us—the Man for others. For him the Lordship of Christ has to do with "down-to-earthness; here-and-now-ness; kairos overriding chronos, appointed time overruling linear time"—that "now is the time of our life.")

PW: *What kind of texts do you hope to write in the future?*

FK: I would hope to be able to write many more hymns that deal honestly (without becoming argumentative, polemic, or nonpoetic) with modern Christians and "fringe-Christians" trying to define their faith and to make their responses to God. Here's an example.

A Hymn of Grateful Recall and Renewed Commitment

For all who have enriched our lives,
    whom we have loved and known,
for saints alive among us still,
    by whom our faith is honed,
we thank you, God, who came and comes
    through women, children, men,
to share the highs and lows of life:
God-for-us, now as then.

For all who with disarming love
    have led us to explore
the risk of reasoning and doubt,
    new realms not known before,
we thank you, God, who came and comes
    to free us from our past,
from ghettos of a rigid mind,
from truths unfit to last.

For all whose laughter has unnerved
    tradition gone awry,
who with incisive gentleness
    pursue each human "why?",
we thank you, God, who came and comes
    to those who probe and ask,
who seek to know the mind of Christ,
and take the church to task.

Now for each other and ourselves
    we pray that, healed of fear,
we may re-live the love of Christ,
    prepared in hope to err.
Then leave us, God, who comes and goes,
    in human-ness to grow,

to care for people, tend the earth,
—the only earth we know!

I also see future works including attempts at celebration without using the still traditional language our churches tend to use. Also, as a pacifist, I feel the need to articulate my (the church's) commitment to "making, speaking, being peace."

PW: *What do you wish you had not written?*

FK: I'm happy to say that those texts I now wish I had not written have never been published anyway! Especially during my most productive years at the Pilgrim Church, Plymouth, I (we) applied the severest possible criteria for deciding whether a hymn was "in" or "out." Whatever I/we judged was once-only material was quite decisively discarded. I never even kept copies of those texts, not even for curiosity's sake. I believe that, as in the field of the visual arts, there is such a thing as "throw-away" hymnody.

PW: *How do you see the hymn functioning in worship?*

FK: I see the role of the hymn principally as one of helping people to *live* the liturgy and to make their response to God. The worst enemies of hymnody are the lazy and insensitive parsons whose choice of hymns for next Sunday is made within a quarter of an hour. As a regular worshiper at an Anglican church in Birmingham (England!) I despair at the moronic way in which hymns are often just "picked out of a hat" and at the unspeakable dullness of the *New English Hymnal*. I have always said, even in the dim and distant past, when hymn writing wasn't even a "twinkle in my eye," that the ordinary worshiper, looking at the hymnboard before the service, should be able to *see* and *feel* where worship is going to *go* that morning!

PW: *How do you see your influence? Is it regional or broader?*

FK: Erik Routley once generously described me as "the archetypal new European hymn writer ... the most sought after of our modern authors in English." Yet English isn't my mother-or-father tongue. I migrated from Holland to Britain when I was 23. Nevertheless, I find my name coupled with Fred Pratt Green and Brian Wren. Dr. Routley used to call us "the leading triumvirate" of the new English renaissance in hymn writing.

I have also found a wealth of evidence that my influence extends well beyond the English-language area, and that my texts have found a truly ecumenical worldwide echo. They sing my hymns in at least 15 different languages, from Thai to Cantonese, from Hungarian to Icelandic; and I never did anything to promote this. It just happened!

I realize that it was fortuitous that my general ministry should lead me into ecumenical and international fields. (Even that was not of my own choosing. I have never in my life applied for a job.) People simply seemed to like what I wrote: "Kaan beats Watts and Wesley" in the 1971 hymnbook of the United Church of Canada and the Anglican Church of Canada. In the new hymnbook of the United Reformed Church in the United Kingdom, I am "third after Watts and Wesley."

It is for me a constant source of thrill and amazement that wherever I go in the world, I find my words in hymnbooks or on scruffy mimeographed bits of paper, and none of it was due to promotional processes at all. One of my more recent texts, "Put Peace into Each Other's Hands" (*Planting Trees and Sowing Seeds*), I am told, has taken contemporary South Africa "by storm." How, I don't know.

So, I believe I have been influential, ecumenically and internationally, but I have not done anything to make this happen. It remains true what I say to audiences and workshop participants every time I talk about my work as a hymn writer: "You see here before you the most surprised hymn writer in the world."

PW: *How do you see your work in relation to late 20th-century hymnody generally?*

FK: My answer to the last question includes my response to this one. It just *happened* that I have become a member of that group of people who, by the grace of God, have been able to "stir up" 20th-century hymnody.

PW: *What in the current hymn scene gratifies you?*

FK: It pleases me that new mainstream hymnals (with a few minor exceptions) coming out these days are more adventurously than in the past willing to make space for contemporary hymnody, and willing to take the risk of including material that may (or may not!) be part of the hymnody of tomorrow's church. It gratifies me (*your* word) that modern hymbooks are honest enough to include pieces that struggle with the faith, and with the church's response to the call of God.

PW: *What in the current scene alarms you?*

FK: What alarms me is the trite, chorus-type, shallow evangelical, musically, poetically, and theologically unadventurous material that is being propagated with great commercial zeal by status-quo Christians. May God forgive us our "fast food" approach to the gospel! I am alarmed by facile, other-worldly discipleship which *is* no discipleship. I am frightened by the rifle association at prayer.

PW: *What does the future of American/English hymnody hold?*

FK: If hymnody in America and England has the courage to respond to its prophetic call, then the very world in which we live will be capable of being changed. If not, God help us. If hymnody does not—without guile, but with "incisive gentleness"—tackle the evils of our time, then the church will become even more meaningless than it often is.

The other thing which *has* to occur is that American/English hymnody not be an isolated thing. It should not have a monopoly on today's *oikoumene* (Greek for "inhabited world"). Any restrictive "trade practice" whereby third-world hymnody is kept out of the English speaking church is in conflict with the gospel.

PW: *What do you regard as the three (or two or one) most representative hymns you have written?*

FK: "For the Healing of the Nations," "Put Peace into Each Other's Hands," and "If You Have Ears, Then Listen."

PW: *How do you feel you have been treated by hymnal editors?*

FK: Well!—especially by George Shorney of Hope Publishing Company who has been fair, creative, and business like. He has also become a good personal friend.

PW: *What or who influenced you? Why do you write hymns?*

FK: I have been influenced by many of today's theologians and poets. My international ministry has enabled me to meet many of them in some 80 different countries. I owe them my gratitude. Juergen Multmann is among my top five, as is the late Norman Goodall, that great ecumenical saint.

       I write hymns because I *have* to. I feel hymn writing is part of a kind of protest movement in the two senses of that word: *against* mealy-mouthed, center-of-the-road (upper) middle class unimaginative Christianity, and *for* (*pro*-test, testifying in favor of) a passionate longing for the kingdom of God *realized* (made real!) here and now, on *this* earth—the only earth we know. The very doctrines of the creation and the incarnation point to what we owe this world and the human family.

PW: *What process do you follow when writing?*

FK: Knowing no music at all, I allow myself to be guided by rhythm and meter. There is a lot of foot-tapping going on in my study when I am writing! I then "waste" pages and pages of A4 (quarto-size European paper), and in the process I keep underlining ideas that may survive. In the end, I am left with the distillation of five to six pages of "attempts." I then pull them together, as it were, "hoping for the best."

> If you have ears, then listen
>   to what the Spirit says
> and give an open hearing
>   to wonder and surprise.
>
> If you have eyes for seeing
>   the word in human form,
> then let your love be telling
>   and your compassion warm.
>
> If you have buds for tasting
>   the apple of God's eye,
> then go, enjoy creation
>   and people on the way.

FRED KAAN

If you have hands for caring,
    then pray that you may know
the tender art of loving
    our world of touch and go

If you can smell the perfume
    of life, the feast of earth,
then sow the seeds of laughter
    and tend the shoots of mirth.

Come, people, to your senses
    and celebrate the day!
For God gives wine for water
    the gift of light for grey.

CHAPTER 8

Erik Routley

All who love and serve your city,
    all who bear its daily stress,
all who cry for peace and justice,
    all who curse and all who bless.

in your day of loss and sorrow,
    in your day of helpless strife,
honor, peace, and love retreating,
    seek the Lord, who is your life.

In your day of wealth and plenty,
    wasted work and wasted play,
call to mind the word of Jesus
    "I must work while it is day."

For all days are days of judgment,
    and the Lord is waiting still,
drawing near a world that spurns him,
    offering peace from Calvary's hill.

Risen Lord! shall yet the city
    be the city of despair?
Come today, our Judge, our Glory;
    be its name, "The Lord is there!"

Biographical Sketch

Erik Routley (1917–82) was born in Brighton, Sussex, England, to John and Eleanor Routley on October 31, 1917. He attended Lancing College, a preparatory school, then went to Magdalen College, Oxford, where in 1940 he received the B.A. in Classics. Three years later he received the M.A. from Oxford and was also ordained to the ministry of the Congregational Church which was then known as the Congregational Union of England and Wales.

In 1944, he married Margaret Scott. Two years later he completed the B.D. at Oxford with a thesis on church music and theology which was later published as *The Church and Music*. The next year his son Nicholas was born, and two years later his son Patrick. In 1952 he received the Ph.D. from Oxford with a dissertation later titled *The Music of Christian Hymnody,* when it was published in a considerably shortened version with many examples excised. A year later his daughter Priscilla was born.

From 1943 to 1974, with the exception of an eleven year interval, Routley served as a pastor in Wednesbury, Dartford, Edinburgh, and New Castle upon Tyne. During the eleven-year interval from 1948 to 1959, between the Dartford and Edinburgh pastorates, he was lecturer in Church History, Librarian, Chaplain, and Director of Music at Mansfield College, Oxford.

From 1948 until 1974 Routley edited *The Bulletin of the Hymn Society of Great Britain and Ireland*. Elected President of the Oxford Organists' Association in 1950, in 1951 he founded the Guild of Congregational Organists and served as its President until 1959. He was reelected in 1970, the same year he was president of his church body. When that church became part of the United Reformed Church in 1972, he was made chairman of the newly-formed Doctrine and Worship Committee. In 1965 he was made a Fellow of the Royal School of Church Music.

A prolific writer and lecturer, between 1962 and 1975 he visited the United States repeatedly, often speaking at seminaries. These trips included the Stone Lectures at Princeton Seminary and the Gheens Lectures at Louisville Seminary, both of which resulted in books. During the 1960s he also sparked the Dunblane meetings about hymnody which set off the hymn explosion of the latter part of this century.

In 1975 he moved to the United States and became Professor of Church Music at Westminster Choir College in Princeton, New Jersey. He continued his whirlwind writing and editing, leading workshops and hymn festivals and preaching and lecturing throughout the country. He died in Nashville, Tennessee, on October 8, 1982.

At his memorial service at Westminster Abbey the following February 8, George Caird, Professor of Exegesis of Holy Scripture at Oxford University, pointed to three characteristics of Routley: his vitality, his memory, and his wit. As to the first, in addition to his pastoral, teaching, editorial and leadership responsibilities, he managed "to write 37 books ... to lecture far and wide on church music, and to compose." As to the second, "his memory was almost freakish." He remembered phone numbers and addresses and dates, and "he knew not only the number of every hymn in all the hymnbooks in common use, but also the tune each hymn was set to, the key, and whether the harmonies had been altered." Yet, even more remarkably, he saw "things in their wholeness." As to the third, "he had that wit which can encapsulate an idea in a telling phrase ... yet his wit was never unkind. His barbed arrows stuck in the mind without ever causing a wound."

Publications

Hymns and Human Life. London: Murry, 1952; and New York: Philisophical Library 1953.

___second edition, with new preface. London: Murray, 1959; Grand Rapids, MI: Eerdmans, 1968.

Hymns and the Faith. London: Murray, 1955; Greenwich, CT: Seabury, 1956; Grand Rapids, MI: Eerdmans, 1968.

The Music of Christian Hymnody: a study of the development of the hymn tune since the Reformation, with special reference to English Protestantism. London: Independent, 1957. Partially based on Routley's Ph.D. dissertation.

The English Carol. London: Jenkins, 1958; New York: Oxford University Press, 1959; Westport, CT: Greenwood, 1973.

Church Music and Theology. London: SCM, 1959; Philadelphia, PA: Muhlenberg, 1959.

___second edition, with new preface. London: Waltham Forest Books, 1965; Philadelphia, PA: Fortress, 1965.

Church Music and the Christian Faith. Carol Stream: Agape, 1978, rewritten version of *Church Music and Theology*.

Hymns Today and Tomorrow. New York: Abingdon, 1964; London: Darton, Longman and Todd, 1966.

An English-Speaking Hymnal Guide. Collegeville, MN: The Liturgical Press, 1979, Chicago: GIA Publications, 1984.

A Panorama of Christian Hymnody. Collegeville, MN: The Liturgical Press, 1979; Chicago: GIA Publications, 1984.

The Music of Christian Hymns. Chicago: GIA Publications, 1981.

Christian Hymns Observed: when in our music God is glorified. Princeton, NJ: Prestige, 1982.

Hymns

(This list is an alphabetized version of the hymns by Routley given in *Duty and Delight: Routley Remembered,* ed. Robin A. Leaver and James H. Litton. Carol Stream: Hope, 1985, 272–74. Routley's texts and tunes are collected in *Our Lives Be Priase* [Carol Stream: Hope, 1990].)

All who love and serve your city

Christ, gladdening light of holy glory
Christ is risen, death is vanquished
Christ, the Church's Lord

Father, with all your gospel's power

Gladly to God's holy temple
God is love: God is light
God is love, God is love
God, omnipotent, eternal
God shows the way to heaven
God speaks, and all things come to be
Go in peace, and God be with you
Good Spirit of God, guide of your children
Grant this to me, Lord: let me live

ERIK ROUTLEY

Happy is he who walks in God's wise way
High on the mountain Moses prayed

If I today have grieved my Saviour's heart
In praise of God meet duty and delight

Keep in mind that Jesus Christ is now risen

Light and salt you call your friends

New songs of celebration render

O mighty God! Creator and Redeemer
Our Jesus is Saviour, Lord and friend

Praise God, peace to all men
Praise the Father in his holy place
Praise to you, Jesus Christ

Seeking water, seeking shelter
Surprised by joy no song can tell

The earth is the Lord's and its fulness
There in God's garden stands the tree of wisdom

We have one Lord
What if someone had recognized us
When the wind caresses the waves of the sea
Where am I? Lost am I!

Interview

(Author's note: Since Erik Routley cannot be interviewed, we reprint here "The Nature of Hymnody" which is the first chapter of Erik Routley, *Christian Hymns Observed: When in Our Music God Is Glorified* [Princeton: Prestige Publications, Inc., 1982], pp. 1–6.)

Hymns are delightful and dangerous things. They are regarded, in the late twentieth century, as inseparable from the worship of all but a very few Christian groups. They are as familiar an activity as reading a newspaper; in worship they are for many people the most intelligible and agreeable of all the activities they are invited to join in or to witness; they are the most easily memorized of all Christian statements, and one who has not been in a church for most of a lifetime, but who was brought up in church when young, remembers some hymns, though everything else may be forgotten.

Hymns are a kind of song: but they differ from a professional song, or an art-song, in being songs for unmusical people to sing together. They are a kind of poetry, but they are such poetry as unliterary people can utter together. The music carries the poetry into the mind and experience; and if the poetry is too weighty for the music to get it moving, it won't move; while if the music is so eloquent as to drown the sound of the words, the words, no matter what nonsense they may talk, will go clear past the critical faculty into the affections.

Hymns, being communal song, have a good deal in common with folk song. So let us for a moment consider folk song. Folk song is that kind of song which people sing without any concern with who its composer was, or of the age from which it came: that is, without critical concern and without the kind of appreciation a professional brings to the contemplation of music. True, many folk songs are recognized by cultivated musicians as being of great beauty—but whereas some kinds of music can speak only to those who are well trained in music's language, true folk song speaks to all.

Secular folk song goes with words concerned with the things that mean most to a community. Basically these are love, work and death. Folk song universalizes these experiences; it objectifies them, and by so doing detaches the singer from the anxieties which all three inevitably carry; the music and the verse smooth the asperities of the basic experiences of life, make them friendly and tractable. A folk song can handle everything from high humor to high tragedy but when it does that, it makes life's incongruities and anomalies entertaining by transforming them into humor, and life's griefs less oppressive by allowing the singer to stand away from them and, obscurely no doubt but none the less assuredly, to feel that the burden is shared by humanity.

One form of folk song is the work song—the sea shanty, let us say—the song adapted to the rhythms of hauling up sails or turning a capstan. Such songs have now gone into history with the disappearance of sails and capstans: but the rhythm of the song, and the narrative of the crude verse, laced with bawdiness quite often, together with the burden, or chorus, in which everybody who had breath to spare could join, eased the rigor of the work and made its drudgery friendly: that is a parable of what all folk song ever did, whether or not it was associated with muscular and physical work.

When we speak of folk song now we still mean songs which have survived through many generations and whose origins are buried in mystery. But of course there are folk songs whose origins are perfectly discoverable and may be quite recent. As soon as a song becomes the property of people who are not musical, as soon as it can be sung, and is sung, by people who are not in any sense natural singers (still less professional ones) it is a folk song. It happens that our present age is so sated with so vast a deluge of public music that it is difficult for any song to rise to the top—the crowd jostles too much further down. People whistle a good deal less than they used to. But right up to the days of the First World War folk song flourished in this sense. It could be fashioned out of what began as 'serious' music, like 'Land of Hope and Glory'; it could emerge from goodness knew where, like 'Pack up your troubles': it could be composed by an identifiable composer like Stephen Foster. Indeed, there were, during the early age of new-style popular music, plenty of tunes of Noel Coward's that came close to achieving folk-song status—and of Cole Porter's. It is an accident—one hopes, a recoverable one—though nobody can be optimistic about that just now, that the music with which ordinary folk are bombarded in modern society is either so sophisticated and ingenious in its vulgarity, or associated, as are the ubiquitous commercials of the advertising media, with such dubious purposes, that ours happens to be an age in which it is necessary to explain the nature of folk song at all.

But there is no question that some hymns have achieved folk-song standing. "Amazing Grace," for example: this is now a secular folk song, in as much as it is often sung in contexts in which the import of the phrase "Amazing Grace" has no meaning and by people who have, and want to have, no conception of what they are singing about. The same could be said of "Morning has broken," another casualty of the media-age,—though apart from the fact that it seems to be heard quite acceptably at any time of day or night, one has to admit that its text doesn't lose much if nobody attends to it. The association of "Abide with me" and the Welsh tune CWM RHONDDA with football matches (and they are now usually solos or choral numbers rather than joined in by all present on such occasions) has given them a folk-song standing.

It looks then from what we have just said as if we are going to argue that folk song is a poor relation of hymnody, or of poetry and music in general; we have said, and we shall indeed insist on saying, that the hymns we have mentioned have been debased, and in some cases fatally damaged, by becoming folk songs. But in fact we are going to say something quite different, and we must at once clear up what will otherwise be a confusion and a contradiction.

Hymns are the folk song of the Christian folk. But the Christian folk is a very odd creature indeed. Recall what we said a minute ago. Folk song celebrates what means most to the folk. That is true of hymns. So if you know what hymns a person loves most, or what hymns a congregation is most addicted to, you will be able to infer what, in Christianity, means most to that person or that church. And that inference won't be speculative: it will be perfectly sound.

You are entitled to say that when people sing hymns they don't pay much attention to the words they sing, and that their satisfaction is usually generated by the tune rather than the text. In as much as that is true, it is a degeneration (as we shall show) from an earlier state of things: but if we have to accept it, then we shall be obliged to judge the content of a person's or a group's faith by the music perhaps more than by the words they sing in their hymns. So be it; it makes life a little more difficult because the judgment we have just said if a valid one requires some musical expertness before it can be made. But the fact is that words still mean a good deal; or if they don't, once the music has carried them past the critical faculty into the affections, they do a certain amount of good or harm.

116

Notice at this point two odd things about this kind of folk song. In the first place, there are sensitive people who have declared their extreme dislike of hymns: the most eloquent and eminent of these is the late C. S. Lewis to whom we shall return later; but the whole Quaker tradition, which is a culture of responsible, orderly and sensitive minds, is against communal hymn singing in their central acts of worship. 'Hymn-singing' or 'psalm-singing,' used as an adjective, was at one time a very commonly accepted epithet of abuse as applied to the pious. Associated with this is the other point: hymn-lovers and hymn-critics often speak of bad hymns as distinguished from good ones. Who ever spoke of a bad sea shanty, or a bad medieval carol? (One species of folk song, the nursery rhyme, has evoked from enlightened educationists' criticisms in this or that case of a rhyme, like 'Dong Dong Bell, Pussy's in the well,' which they deem to be conducive to unacceptable moral standards in young children: but that is an unusual case and statements of it are usually loaded with a good deal of overkill: there are people who would say we shouldn't sing the Twenty-third Psalm because it is insulting to call people sheep.)

Something has come into sight which we must identify. There is some quality about Christian folk songs that makes them vulnerable to corruption in a sense in which secular folk songs aren't.

Well: the fact (which few people have noticed, or anyhow commented on) is that Christianity is as fatally *imitable* as the music of Handel. Any musician knows how in the English eighteenth century music took on a fatal facility and garrulousness which it took a Vaughan Williams to identify, diagnose, and dissipate. That was, it is hardly unfair to say, because everybody thought they could write like Handel (or, on the continent, like the pupils of Bach). There was a new market for it, and the hacks were ready to meet the demand. In the same way there have always been imitations of Christianity (which had in common with the real thing only those aspects of the real thing which appeal to the unregenerate nature) that have never failed to win a measure of popular approval. I shall be obliged to refer later on to the evangelical tyranny of Count Nicolas von Zinzendorf, and I shall have to cause my readers and myself the embarrassment of referring to contemporary versions of that. There have been power-seeking imitations of Christianity, and moralistic imitations, and pseudo-mystical imitations, and pseudo-poetic imitations, and organization-minded imitations, and even ecumenical imitations—and they all have this in common with each other, that any attempt to criticize them is always made to reflect on the critic, and to justify the attribution to him of looseness of faith, hostility to the truth, and a general beastliness of nature. They also have this in common—that they have parted company with reason, and that they have renounced penitence: but it is never any use saying so. It is, one has to say, fatally easy to imitate or travesty Christianity.

Well, hymnody is the folk song of *that*—of the Faith in all its austerity and grandeur here, and of the imitation in all its attractiveness there. We have to take it as we find it, and obviously in a short book it will be sensible to concentrate on what seems to reflect the authentic innocent beauty of the Christian faith and style. But we may as well know what we are in for.

Hymn singing is nowadays thought of as a communal or congregational activity, and we should be disposed to define a hymn as a strophic song on a Christian subject capable of being sung by a congregation which was not in any sense made up of trained singers. But any definition in terms of that kind would be narrower than the original definition of a hymn, which is simply a song of praise. 'Hymn' is a Greek word, in use long before the Christian era. A hymn need not, on that primitive definition, be religious and it need not be communally sung: therefore obviously it need not be strophic. It is no more than a song of a serious kind making use of poetry and music in a way which tends to exalt the mind of the singer and listener towards lofty subjects—whatever subject may be recognized by that particular community as lofty. In Christian use, 'Hymn' has not necessarily meant a congregational song: indeed for three quarters of the time that Christianity has been in the world it meant, as we shall see in a moment, precisely not that. And even during the time when congregational singing was familiar in church (that is, after the Reformation) 'Hymn' can mean a choral piece performed to a listening congregation.

It is as well to remember that, even though the subject of this book is in fact congregational hymnody. For as long as hymnody is not the property of an uncritical congregation, it is subject only to the disciplines of music and poetry and, if it is Christian, Christian theology. As soon as it falls into the hands of people whose chief business is not thinking about poetry and music, it tends to require other forms of discipline, and from time to time the Church has applied it, with greater or less success.

But in more recent times—broadly speaking, during the century now nearing its end—the idea of 'a good hymn' and 'a bad hymn,' the self-conscious criticism and investigation of hymns according to the disciplines of literature, music and theology, has become an accepted study, and that is known as hymnology. There has always been criticism of the use of music in church, and authorities from time to time have warned the church against its incongruous, unseasonable or extravagant use: that is not hymnology because what is said in such warnings can just as well be said about organ voluntaries or anthems as about hymns. Hymnology is a subject which shares frontiers with several others—like one of those small counties in England which local government reconstruction has swept away and which, in themselves of limited area, border on several other larger regions. Hymnology has a common boundary with musicology, with literary criticism, with theology and with sociology; it is the study of what people do when for most of the time they hardly know they are doing it, and the application to that study of the principles of larger and more definable disciplines. That sort of activity has been going on for just about a hundred years—not more. These pages are a contribution to it, on the scale, perhaps, of the operations of a specialized ecologist studying an acre or two in what is anyhow quite a small county.

I would myself insist that it is a kind of ecology—the study of living things living with each other: of people living with the church and with music and with poetry and with doctrine; primarily, of people and groups of people.

And most of the time we shall find ourselves looking at the church in times of crisis and of tension. Not that the church has spent much of its time in any other condition—but hymns, we shall find, have flourished most vigorously on the far edges of the church: at what some might call its growing points and others its vulnerable or even heretical points. The pattern forms itself at once: periods when somebody somewhere is tearing up the turf and asking ques-

tions and organizing rebellions and reconstructing disciplines produce hymns: when the steam goes out of such movements, or they
become part of an expanded main stream, hymn writing goes on
in a more tranquil way, but never for very long. Another colour is
added to the picture by another 'movement' and that movement
brings new hymns and new kinds of hymn into the repertory. That
is what we shall be noticing as soon as we start the journey.

New songs of celebration render
    to him who has great wonders done;
awed by his love his foes surrender
    and fall before the Mighty one.

He has made known his great salvation
    which all his friends with joy confess;
he has revealed to every nation
    his everlasting righteousness.

Joyfully, heartily resounding,
    let every instrument and voice
peal out the praise of grace abounding,
    calling the whole world to rejoice.

Trumpets and organs set in motion
    such sounds as make the heavens ring:
all things that live in earth and ocean,
    make music for your mighty King.

Rivers and seas and torrents roaring,
    honor the Lord with wild acclaim;
mountains and stones look up adoring
    and find a voice to praise his Name.

Righteous, commanding, ever glorious,
    praises be his that never cease;
just is our God, whose truth victorious
    establishes the world in peace.

CHAPTER 9

Thomas H. Troeger

"Silence! Frenzied, unclean spirit,"
    cried God's healing, Holy One.
"Cease your ranting! Flesh can't bear it.
    "Flee as night before the sun."
At Christ's voice the demon trembled,
    from its victim madly rushed,
while the crowd that was assembled
    stood in wonder, stunned and hushed.

Lord, the demons still are thriving
    in the grey cells of the mind:
tyrant voices, shrill and driving,
    twisted thoughts that grip and bind,
doubts that stir the heart to panic,
    fears distorting reason's sight,
guilt that makes our loving frantic,
    dreams that cloud the soul with fright.

Silence, Lord, the unclean spirit,
    in our mind and in our heart.
Speak your word that when we hear it
    all our demons shall depart.
Clear our thought and calm our feeling,
    still the fractured, warring soul.
By the power of your healing
    make us faithful, true, and whole.

Biographical Sketch

Thomas Troeger was born on January 30, 1945 in Suffern, New York, and considers Cooperstown, New York, his home town. He was raised on daily Bible readings, great English poetry (especially the romantics), and the music of Bach, Handel, Haydn, and Mozart.

Church from his earliest years was a positive experience for him. He sang in the children's choir, attended Christian education programs, heard great preaching, participated in enthusiastic hymn singing, and often played the flute in his own and many other churches.

Throughout high school he studied flute with John Oberbrunner of the Syracuse School of Music and dreamed about being a professional flutist. Under the impact of his pastor's preaching, however, he decided to become a minister—or perhaps to teach English literature because of his love for poetry which was fed by his English teacher, Ruth Yule.

He went to Yale as an English major who also studied quite a bit of Philosophy and German, and graduated with a B.A. *cum laude* in 1967. He continued playing the flute and performed a considerable amount of chamber music with Robert Conant, harpsichordist.

He attended Colgate Rochester Divinity School where he received the B.D. in 1970. While there he was immersed in African American preaching and worship. The fervor of the preaching and the power of the music expanded and deepened the passion he already felt for the music and worship of his own tradition. That fusion of different cultures and styles became a central spiritual dynamic in his faith, one which continues to the present.

Troeger was Associate Pastor for seven years at New Hartford Presbyterian Church, from 1970 to 1977. He thought he would never leave the pastorate because he worked with a creative colleague, Richard Manzelmann, and because the church and community were so responsive to their collaborative ministry.

In 1977, however, Colgate Rochester invited him to return to teach preaching and parish ministry. Wanting more time to write, he accepted. He had already published his first book, *Meditation: Escape to Reality,* which traced the relationship of hatha yoga to western prayer disciplines. Two more books were about to appear.

At Colgate Rochester Troeger immediately began working with Carol Doran, the pastoral musician, an individual Troeger regards as an extraordinary talent and well-practiced in a wide range of church music. Their work together and their dream of a new kind of hymnody started Troeger writing hymns.

He also began to write in the fields of homiletics and liturgics, with a special focus on the imaginative and visionary capabilities of preachers. This further stimulated his hymn writing. His first homiletics book, *Creating Fresh Images for Preaching,* is highly poetic in style and was voted one of the 10 most important books of 1982 by the Academy of Parish Clergy.

In 1991 Troeger became the Peck professor of preaching and communications at Iliff School of Theology in Denver. There he began to collaborate with another "brilliant" musician, John Kuzma. Troeger and Kuzma have created hymns, a set of mystical anthems, an art song cycle, a secular cantata, and a miniature opera. A grand opera is in progress.

Troeger is a member of the North American Academy of Liturgy, The Hymn Society in the United States and Canada, and the Academy of Homiletics of which he was president in 1987. He is married to Merle Marie Troeger.

Publications

Books

Borrowed Light: Hymn Texts, Prayers, and Poems. New York: Oxford University Press, 1994.

New Hymns for the Lectionary: To Glorify the Maker's Name. With Carol Doran. New York: Oxford University Press, 1986.

New Hymns for the Life of the Church: To Make Our Prayer and Music One. With Carol Doran. New York: Oxford University Press, 1992.

Open to Glory: Renewing Worship in the Congregation. With Carol Doran. Valley Forge: Judson Press, 1983.

Contributor to

The Hymnological Annual, an International Forum on the hymn and Worship. Ed. Vernon Wicker. Berreine Springs: Vande Vere Publishing Ltd., 1991.

The inclusive language liturgical psalter of the International Commission on English and the Liturgy.

Editor

Art and media editor for the journal, *Homiletic.*

Editorial board of *Worship.*

Articles

"Advent Reflections and Resources," with Carol Doran, *Word and Witness* 8:1(A) (1983), 1–4.

"Art in Worship: The Integrity of Form and Feeling," *Reformed Liturgy and Music,* 17 (Summer, 1983), 122–25.

"Art and Media," *Homiletic* 12:2 (1987), 27–31.

"Good Friday," *Word and Witness* 9:4 (37) (April 5, 1985), 1–4.

"The Hidden Stream that Feeds: Hymns As a Resource for the Preacher's Imagination," *The Hymn* 43:3 (July 1992), 16–23.

"Overhearing Love's Music in a Brutal World," *Preaching through the Apocalypse. Sermons from Revelation.* Ed. Cornish R. Rogers and Joseph R. Jeter. (St. Louis: Chalice Press), 97–105.

"Personal, Cultural and Theological Influences on the Language of Hymns and Worship," *The Hymn* 38:4 (October, 1987), 7–16.

"Recognizing an Ancient Unity: Music and Liturgy as Complemental Disciplines," with Carol Doran, *Worship* 60:5 (September, 1986), 386–98.

"Writing Hymns as a Theologically Informed Artistic Discipline," with Carol Doran, *The Hymn* 36:2 (April, 1985), 7–11.

THOMAS H. TROEGER

Hymns and Lyric Poems

A cheering, chanting, dizzy crowd
A fixed sum
A single leaf
A single unmatched stone
A spendthrift lover is the Lord
A star not mapped on human charts
All that rises toward the sky
As a chalice cast of gold
As servants working an estate
As trees that withstand the wind's shaking
Ask, seek, knock

Before the fruit is ripened by the sun
Before the temple's great stone sill
Beyond the press and pull of crowds
Blessed be you, O God

Come singing, come singing
Creator of all that is
Crown as your king the King who came crownless
Crucified Savior

Density of light
Direct us, Lord, through darkness

Eagles' spiralings comply

Far easier to melt the gold
Far from the markets of rich meat and wine
Far more than passion's passing flame
Fierce the force that curled Cain's fist
First the wind upon the water
Forever in the heart there springs
From Pharaoh to King Cyrus

Gangling desert birds will sing
Glory to God is the song of the stars

127

WITH TONGUES OF FIRE

God folds the mountains out of rock
Go forth with the blessing of God
God made from one blood all the families of earth
God marked a line and told the sea
God of Gabriel
God of mercy and compassion
God, you move among us with grace

Has it been that long?
Heart, hold fast
Holy and good is the gift of desire
How buoyant and bold the stride of Christ's friends
How long, O Lord, how long?
How unlike all earthly glory

I open the black cupboard door, a single wide warped plank
I walk the farm I never walked
I'd lie in bed if lying still I'd sleep
If all you want, Lord, is my heart
If Christ is charged with madness
If winter never spiked and stunned
In shade I watch my neighbor in the sun
In the babble of a baby
Instead of a king
It used to be that the island of sand
It's not because archbishops

Kneeling in the garden grass

Let all who pray the prayer Christ taught
Let the Truth shine in our speaking
Lions and oxen will feed in the hay
Listen to the cloud that brightens

Make our church one joyful choir
Make your prayer and music one
May the God whose music sounded

Neither desert wind nor sun
No dusk, but sudden night
No iron spike, no granite weight

O gracious Christ
O gracious power
O praise the gracious power
On a visit south in January
On bringing a friend purple tulips
On the sand, in the sun
Our founders cleared an open field
Our Savior's infant cries were heard
Our Shepherd is the Lamb

Pastor, lead our circle dance
Pounding a nail in my cellar shop
Praise the Source of faith and learning
Praise to the Spinner who twisted and twirled

Risen Christ, may death be swift

Searcher of human hearts
Seek for the kingdom with all of your powers
Seek not in distant, ancient hills
Set free, set free by God's grace
Silence! frenzied, unclean spirit
Sing with Gabriel the greeting
Soundless were the tossing trees
Source and sovereign of all creation
Source and sovereign, rock and cloud
Startled by a holy humming
Suddenly God's sovereign wind
Swiftly pass the clouds of glory

The ballad of the woman bent double
The beauty of the sound of the bells
The branch that bends with clustered fruit
The bush in flame but not consumed

WITH TONGUES OF FIRE

The Christians traveled Caesar's roads
The cross on the hill is the measuring rod
The faith we sing was sown
The first day of creation
The hands that first held Mary's child
The hidden stream that feeds
The least in God's kingdom is greater than John
The leper's soul was no less scarred
The lick of the tide, the lunge of the storm
The love that lifted lyric praise
The moon with borrowed light
The rocks would shout if we kept still
The sails were spilling wind
The scantiest touch of grace can heal
The sheep stood stunned in sudden light
The song and prayer of birds
The Word of God was from the start
These things did Thomas count as real
Though every sun shall spend its fire
Through our fragmentary prayers
To those who knotted nets of twine
Too splendid for speech but ripe for a song
Twenty-five years

Unbidden came God's love
Unless this day be holy

View the present through the promise

Water moving through stone
We have the strength to lift and bear
We need each other's voice to sing
We travel toward a land unknown
What fabled names from Judah's past
What king would wade through murky streams
When heaven's voice was still
When there is no star to guide you
Where mountains lift the eye

THOMAS H. TROEGER

Wherever there Are tyrant voices
While the court and priests conspire
Who commands vast worlds in motion?
Why stare at heaven's distant blue?
Wild the man and wild the place
Wind who makes all winds that blow
With glad, exuberant carolings
With pipes of tin and wood make known
Writing at dusk

Interview

PW: *Could you give some sense of your theological accents?*

TT: I write for thinking people of faith who have a passion for beauty because it empowers them to do justice and embody the gospel in their lives. I abhor and detest literalism, anti-aestheticism, and anti-intellectualism. My spirit is crushed when these are manifest in the church and in the proclamation of the gospel. I consciously write to counter these diabolical characteristics of some religious practice and belief.

I work to incorporate the insights of biblical scholarship and 20th-century theologians who are helping us to understand what it means to be Christian in a global community. I also strive to make my language beautiful, something that one would want to sing or read again after a service because of the delight of the sound and the play of the imagery. I am convinced that the reason the most beloved passages of the Bible (for example, Psalm 23, the prolog to John, and 1 Corinthians 13) are so beloved is because they are a fusion of magnificent language and thought. Therefore, I love to work with those time-honored poetic devices which still have the capacity to stir the heart—rhyme, meter, assonance, alliteration, and startling imagery. At the same time, I strive for diction that is not antiquated. Hymns of poetic splendor are theology in ecstasy, and even though I may often fail to reach that goal, it is the mark toward which I aim.

My hymns tend to draw their inspiration from two major sources: specific biblical passages and contemporary needs.

They evince a range of Christogical understandings. They often deal with the heart and the inner life, not as a way of escape from the world, but because I believe that being transformed by the grace of God is essential to the transformation of the world.

My hymns are often apologetic in the classic theological sense of that word: interpreting faith to a culture that is not easily able to grasp its meaning.

PW: *What do you hope to write in the future?*

TT: I am currently working on a grand opera and art songs which present the meaning of faith in ways that will make sense to people who stand on the periphery of belief and who seldom or never come to church, often for excellent reasons. My goal along with the composer, John Kuzma, is to develop a poetic/musical idiom that conveys the hidden workings of grace to people who fear that traditional religious language and piety will choke their intellect and imagination.

PW: *Is there anything you now wish you had not written?*

TT: There are, of course, hymnpoems (I made up this noun to bypass the silly debates about if hymns are poems) that I count less than successful, if not downright bad. But I am not sure that I wish I had not written them. It is often working through the bad stuff that brings a writer to the good stuff, and that is as true for me as for any other writer.

PW: *How do you see the hymn functioning in worship?*

TT: The answer has to be wide ranging because there are so many different functions depending on its placement in the liturgy and what the theological/liturgical/pastoral need is. There are times of our totally abandoning ourselves in the glad rhapsodic praise of God, and some exuberant hymn can be the vehicle of such adoration. But then there are other moments of confession or quiet introspection that require a completely different kind of hymn. And still others when we are wanting to send people out with a sense of empowerment for their daily ministries in the world.

I suppose we might summarize these varied needs into a principle: The hymn should function as the best possible expression of the community's prayer for that place in the liturgy for which it is chosen. This principle means it can never be chosen in isolation without consideration of its immediate liturgical context.

PW: *How do you perceive your influence? Is it regional or more broad than that?*

TT: I am not certain what to say on this. I do know that I have received correspondence and/or settings of my texts not only from North America and Great Britain, but also Tanzania, Germany, Australia, and Japan. And I have read reviews in a wide range of journals. Also, other poets have sent me pieces that they say were inspired by my work, or they send collections of their own hymns seeking my critical assessment.

When I received an honorary doctorate of sacred theology from Dickinson College in May of 1993, the significance of my work as an innovator in hymnody was one of the specific things mentioned in the citation.

I am not sure all this adds up to being "influential," but it suggests my work has more than purely regional influence.

PW: *How do you see your work in relation to late 20th-century hymnody generally?*

TT: My understanding of 20th-century hymnody is that there are so many currents and movements that it would be difficult to summarize in a phrase. I think, for example, of the impact of the charismatic movement, the ostinatos of Taizé, the development of gospel, the introduction of hymns from around the world, Christian songs that fit the broad category of popular music, the serious hymnody of other writers represented in this book, and even the debates in the Hymn Society about what constitutes a hymn, which has direct bearing on what we might include under 20th-century hymnody.

With all of this in mind, I would say my hymnody represents an attempt to draw upon the core traditions of EuroAmerican congregational song while seeking a new idiom that is expressive of the great theological projects of this century: reinterpreting the meaning of faith in a scientific and technological culture, liberating Christianity from distortions of sexism and racism, coming to terms with the ever increasing awareness of other world religions and cultures.

PW: *What in the current hymnic scene gratifies you?*

TT: The sheer richness of what is being created. It is evidence that there are still enormous spiritual energies in the church and the culture.

PW: *Is there anything that is alarming?*

TT: How easily the church will sometimes fall for what is shoddy and superficial.

I am also concerned about the lack of musical and literary education for most people so that there is less and less of the discerning artistic culture that will encourage and sustain the development of liturgical poetry and music that has enduring value.

PW: *What does the future of American/English hymnody hold?*

TT: I believe the most pressing issues will continue to emerge from the shifting state of theology. As we come more and more to terms with other world religions and with the oppressive and distorted ways in which Christian faith is often presented, we will be faced with the question of what kind of conviction, what kind of passion will fuel the writing of hymns in the next century. Can an open, cosmopolitan faith feed an intense enough piety to focus the energy of poets on the creation of hymns? I believe so, but this will be a matter of theological struggle and spiritual questioning. It may be that we will lose our nerve and retreat to a more secure faith, the repetion of past formulae, the disavowal of new idioms of belief, and our hymnody will become religious clubhouse songs that do not empower us to live in the global village. But I am hoping and praying for a more daring and visionary faith, and subsequently a more innovating and courageous hymnody.

PW: *What do you regard as the three (or two or one) most representative hymns you have written?*

TT: "These Things Did Thomas Count as Real," "When There Is No Star to Guide You," and "Where Mountains Lift the Eye."

THOMAS H. TROEGER

PW: *How do you feel you have been treated by hymnal editors?*
TT: Extremely well by my primary editor, Susan Brailove of Oxford University Press, and always with respect and appreciation by other editors.

PW: *What or who influenced you? Why do you write hymns?*
TT: I write hymns because the love of God is beyond all telling of it, yet I must try.

The influences at both a spiritual and technical, artistic level include J. S. Bach and G. F. Handel who made me want to create something beautiful as an expression of my gratitude to God that I should ever have lived to hear music as glorious as what they composed in the praise of God.

Also important: studying closely the texts of Donne, Herbert, Watts, Wesley, Cowper, Hopkins, Hardy, Bishop, Stephens, Frost, Yeats, Eliot, Auden, Wren, Pratt Green, Sexton, Vajda, Larkin, Plath, Dickey, black spirituals, Heaney, Milosz, and others. The list is far longer than this, and always growing.

It is also impossible to overstress the significance of the individuals named in my biographical sketch, particularly the musicians whose art has fed my poetry.

PW: *What process do you follow when writing?*
TT: If I am working from a biblical text, I read it over and over, pray about it, break it apart through literary analysis and often place myself in the role of a character in the text or the original community for whom it was written. Once I get an initial opening line, I sit down and work obsessively at my computer. Then, when it is all done, I often find it is no good, but has a few fine useable lines or possibilities, so I start again. I will work for hours at a stretch, then go for a long walk with a pad and pencil because the thing will often come upon me after I have walked two or three miles.

I frequently consult with the composer of the tune to see how she or he responds to the first stanza and to gain ideas on how it needs to develop.

If the hymn is a commission or on a particular topic, I will often write out in prose what I want to say, including how the poem will develop. Then I put on a Bach cantata or

135

Handel concerto and let the musical sounds condense into hummings in my soul that crystalize over time into words.

And sometimes I am simply seized with a hymnpoem. For example, I wrote "If All You Want, Lord, Is My Heart" in 45 minutes for no other reason than it came upon me.

PW: *Do you want to add anything?*

TT: I am delighted you are doing this book because I believe it is essential that the church take seriously the language it will give people to sing, and the church needs to understand how strenuous the production of quality hymnody is. Thank you.

> The word of God was from the start.
> The word drove seas and land apart.
> The word made rocks and living things.
> The word raised up and brought down kings.
>
> The word became a child of earth.
> The word arrived through human birth.
> The word like us was blood and bone.
> The word knew life as we have known.
>
> The word of God was human sized,
> The word by most unrecognized.
> The word by others was received.
> The word gave life when they believed.
>
> The word had first made flesh and sod,
> The word-made-flesh turned flesh toward God.
> The word is working on flesh still.
> The word is spelling out God's will.
>
> The word shall be our life and light.
> The word shall be our power and might.
> The word above all wealth is priced.
> The word by name is Jesus Christ.

CHAPTER 10
Jaroslav J. Vajda

God of the sparrow
God of the whale
God of the swirling stars
    How does the creature say Awe
    How does the creature say Praise

God of the earthquake
God of the storm
God of the trumpet blast
    How does the creature say Woe
    How does the creature cry Save

God of the rainbow
God of the cross
God of the empty grave
    How does the creature say Grace
    How does the creature say Thanks

God of the hungry
God of the sick
God of the prodigal
    How does the creature say Care
    How does the creature say Life

God of the neighbor
God of the foe
God of the pruning hook
    How does the creature say Love
    How does the creature say Peace

God of the ages
God near at hand
God of the loving heart
    How do Your children say Joy
    How do Your children say Home

Biographical Sketch

Jaroslav Vajda was born in 1919 in Lorain, Ohio, where his father was a Lutheran pastor. His family's roots were in Slovakia, from which all his grandparents emigrated in the 1880s. His parents were born near Hazleton, Pennsylvania. There one grandfather owned a grocery store, and one was a brewmaster in a local brewery. His father graduated from Concordia Theological Seminary in Springfield, Illinois, in 1918, and returned to Hazleton to marry Mary Gecy, a church organist and floorlady in the Hazleton silk mill.

After Ohio, Vajda's father was called to serve churches in Virginia and Wisconsin and then, when Jaroslav was seven, Indiana Harbor (East Chicago), Indiana. There he attended St. Paul Lutheran Elementary School and Washington High School. At the age of 13 he went to Concordia College in Fort Wayne to begin pre-seminary training for the Lutheran ministry.

Vajda immersed himself in his ethnic heritage. He developed a capacity to handle the language. When he was 15, a novelist, an archaeologist and artist, and a historian from the Cultural Institute of Slovakia visited his family in East Chicago. They left books of Slovakia's classic literature. Jaroslav became interested in these books and began translating parts of them into English. The translations grew to 100 poems of Slovak and Czech poets and a 52 sonnet sequence by Slovakia'a greatest poet, Pavol Orszagh Hviezdoslav (1849–1921).

Jaroslav recalls another "impetus" to his hymn writing. *The Cresset* was a Christian magazine of literature and the arts, founded by O. P. Kretzmann, one of the leading literary figures of The Lutheran Church—Missouri Synod in Vajda's youth. At the age of 18, Vajda submitted several poems to *The Cresset*. Kretzmann responded with a note which said, "You have an authentic gift for poetry." Vajda has remarked (in *Now the Joyful Celebration,* p. 7), "I can hardly estimate the effect those seven words had on my determination to write poetry, and eventually, hymns."

In 1945, Vajda graduated from Concordia Theological Seminary in St. Louis, Missouri, married Louise Mastaglio of Milwaukee, and from 1945 until 1963 served three parishes: Trinity Lutheran Church in Cranesville, Pennsylvania; Our Savior Lutheran Church in Alexandria, Indiana; and St. John Lutheran Church in Brackenridge, Penn-

140

sylvania. In 1963 he was appointed the Editor of *This Day,* a Christian monthly family magazine. In 1971 he became book developer/editor for Concordia Publishing House and saw 200 books from "concept to publication."

In the course of all this he wrote and translated numerous hymns, became one of the world's experts on Slovak hymnody and especially the most important Slovak Lutheran hymnal—Juraj Tranovsky's *Cithara Sanctorum* of 1636, and authored or edited a number of books. His B.D. thesis at Concordia Seminary was *A History of the Cithara Sanctorum,* and he is currently at work on the sources of Slovak Lutheran hymnody by examining 1600 hymn texts.

Vajda is a member of the Hymn Society in the United States and Canada and the American Association for the Advancement of Slavic Studies. He was made a Fellow of the Hymn Society in 1988.

The Vajdas have four children: Susan, married to Henry Raedeke, Jr.; Jeremy, married to Teresa Corcoran; Timothy; and Deborah, married to Jeffrey Johnson.

Works

An Anthology of Slovak Literature (co-author, tr. Slovak poetry). Riverside: University Hardcovers, 1976.

Bloody Sonnets (tr. of Hviezdoslav's sonnet sequence). Scranton: Obrana Press, 1950.

Follow the King. St. Louis: Concordia, 1977. (devotions)

A History of the Cithara Sanctorum (B.D. thesis). St. Louis: Concordia Seminary, 1944.

Janko Kral' (tr. Slovak poetry). Bratislava: Tatran, 1972.

Now the Joyful Celebration: Hymns Carols and Songs. St. Louis: Morning Star, 1987.

Slovak Christmas. Rome: Slovak Institute, 1960. (trs. Slovak carols and customs)

Something to Sing About. St. Louis: Concordia, 1990. (study guide)

So Much to Sing About: Hymns Carols and Songs, A Supplement to "Now the Joyful Celebration." St. Louis: Morning Star, 1991.

A Song of Blood (tr. of Hviezdoslav's sonnet sequence). Bratislava: Tatran, 1972.

They Followed the King (devotional sketches; a new edition will appear in 1996 with the title *Men and Women of the Word,* Concordia Publishing House). St. Louis: Concordia, 1963.

Uncompromising Faith (tr. Uhorskai memoirs). St. Louis: Concordia, 1992.

Zuzanka Hraskovie (tr. Gresak operetta libretto). Bratislava: Opus, 1978. Plus countless editorials, editing, and poems scattered in various publications.

Hymns

A comet blazed across the skies
A cuckoo flew out of the wood
A dove flew down from heaven
A woman and a coin
Add one more song
All bless the God of Israel
All glory, praise, and blessing
All things are yours
All who crave a greater measure
Amid the world's bleak wilderness
As once in Eden music filled the air
As out of the stem
Ascending, Christ returns to God
Astonished by your empty tomb

Before the marvel of this night
Before your awesome majesty
Begin the song of glory now
Be happy, saints
Blessed be the precious Baby
Blessed chosen generation

Blessed Jesus, living bread
Break forth in praise to God
Breath of the living God

Catch the Vision! Share the glory!
Christ, around your word assembled
Christ goes before
Christ, the model of the meek
Christians, gather round
Christians, let us remember
Come at the summit of this day
Come in holy awe and truth
Come, Lord Jesus, to this place
Come now, shepherds, quickly come
Count your blessings, O my soul
Creator, Keeper, caring Lord

Dear Father God, we rise to say
Dear little Jesus, we come to your bed
Dearest Lord Jesus, why are you delaying?
Delicate child of royal line

Ever since the Savior came

Faithful Christians, one and all
Far from the time when we were few
For your mercy I implore you
From the shadow of my pain

Gather your children, dear Savior, in peace
Gift of joy
Give glory, all creation
Glorious Jerusalem
Glory be to you, O Father
Go, my children, with my blessing
    (wedding stanza added in *So Much to Sing About*)
God almighty, Lord most holy
God first made a fruitful garden

God has a plan for all
God, my Lord, my strength
God of the sparrow
God the father of us all
God, who built this wondrous planet
God, you made this world a garden
Greet now the swiftly changing year

Hail the Savior's very body
Hear me, help me, gracious Savior
Hear me, O my precious Love
Heaven's dawn is breaking brightly
Heralds of the cross
Here is the living proof, good Lord
Holy Spirit, gift of God
How could I hurt you so?
How lovely and how pleasant
How shall we thank you, Christ our Lord?
How meager and mundane
How pleasant, Lord, when brothers live
Hymn of the night

I have a Father you would like
I praise you, Lord, in every hour
If God is absent, all the cost
In Bethlehem, a wonder
In darkest night
In hopelessness and near despair
In the streets, in home and workplace

Jesus, take us to the mountain
Just as a happy bride

Leap, world, for joy
Let all who captive lie
Let our gladness banish sadness
Let us praise our gracious God
Let us sing with heart and voice

JAROSLAV J. VAJDA

Light the candle
Lo, our Shepherd in a manger
Lo, what a wonder
Lord, as you taught us once to pray
Lord, I must praise you
Lord of lords, adored by angels
Lord, we hold your goodness precious

Make songs of joy
My crown of creation

Now, at the peak of wonder
Now go to sleep
Now shine, bright glow of majesty
Now the silence
Now to the babe so tender

O day of days, the day I found
O dearest friend
O Father, send the Spirit down
O God, eternal Father, Lord
O joyous Christmas night
Oh, what tidings bright
One by one the Spirit calls us
Out of the forest a cuckoo flew
Out to the hills

Pass in review
Peace came to earth
Proclaim to the captives

Readings from Acts, versified
Remember, Lord, the times
Rise up, Bethl'hem shepherds, rise
Rock-a-bye, my dear little boy

See Mary setting out at dawn
See this wonder in the making

Shepherds all, come
Shepherds of Bethlehem
Shine like stars
Since you are risen
Sleep, my little one
Sleep softly, softly, beautiful Jesus
Sleep well, dear heavenly boy
Slumber, lovely Baby
So much to sing about
Someone special
    (stanza for teachers added in *So Much to Sing About*)
Son of God, which Christmas is it?
Source of breath
Spirit God, eternal Word
Stand before me, Lord
Sweetest song of this bright season

Tell us, shepherds, why so joyful
The best of gifts
The friend I need
The house with all its parts
The rescue we were waiting for
The Ordinary in hymn form
Then the glory
This child of ours (revised in *So Much to Sing About*)
This glorious Easter festival
This is a time for banners and bells
    (alternate closing stanza added since *So Much to Sing About*)
This love, O Christ
This touch of love
Though mountains quake and oceans roar
Three angels are singing
To the everlasting hills
Today again, the gift of life

Up, shepherds
Up through endless ranks of angels

JAROSLAV J. VAJDA

Wake, shepherds, awake
Wake to the wonder appearing above
Wake up, brother, listen
Walls crack, the trumpet sounds
Weep with us, Jesus
Welcome in the name of Christ
What are you looking for, Magdalen?
What love, Lord Jesus, that you go
What would the world be like?
When God's dread judgment
When you woke that Thursday morning
Where shepherds lately knelt
Where the swallow makes her nest
Where you are, there is life
While Mary rocks her child to rest
Who could have dreamt a land like this?
Who is this who comes from nowhere?
Who's that sitting on the ground?
Wondering child of God
World, for all your gain and pleasure

You are the king
You are the rock
You are the shepherd
You hear the hungry crying
You, Jesus, are my Shepherd true
You said, pray thus
Your heart, O God, is grieved

Interview

PW: *Could you give some sense of your theological point of view?*
JV: I am a confessional Lutheran, as is evidenced in my hymns.

PW: *What do you hope to write in the future?*
JV: I want to do a complete reference on Slovak Lutheran hymns,
      original and in translation; more translations of Slovak poetry;
      a collection of original poetry and translations; a strong Kyrie;
      and worthy products of commissioned hymns.

PW: Is there anything in your output you wish you'd not written?

JV: Fortunately, what I wish I had not written never was pub-lished, except for some "humorous" doggerel for our prep school paper.

PW: How do you see the hymn functioning in worship?

JV: I see the hymn as an honest confession of faith, as a public response to God's "mighty acts" and grace. It grows out of contemporary circumstances and takes on contemporary yet reverent language. What we need in worship are hymns of depth and growth, not mere emotional gushings and wailings.

PW: How do you perceive your influence? Is it regional or broader than that?

JV: Looking back on the 25th anniversary of "Now the Silence," I see it as the unexpected and unintended watershed for my hymnody, and indirectly for other hymn writing in the last quarter of the 20th-century. In an effort to be relevant to the spiritual needs of my contemporaries with the everlasting Gospel, I have striven to deal with the *Why* and *How* of Chris-tian theology as well as the *What*—in poetic form and lan-guage. By the acceptance of my production, I believe I have moved other hymn writers to do something similar and to offer an alternative to the glut of superficial and repetitious religious phrases and slogans which are so popular, but which do not engage root problems which face the world and the church.

The acceptance of subsequent hymns by *Lutheran Book of Worship* and *Lutheran Worship,* together with a growing use of hymns in domestic Lutheran churches, would seem to indicate a regional influence. The inclusion of hymns in other denominational hymnals in the United States and abroad seems to suggest a broader influence. With one or more hymns now appearing in more than 30 hymnals and hymn collections worldwide, and others being sung individually in additional denominations, their acceptance is growing as they are discovered.

What pleases me most about this growing acceptance is the tacit approval of a scripturally-based and inspired hymnody which responds to the grace and glory of the Triune God.

PW: *How do you see your work in relation to late 20th-century hymnody generally?*

JV: I see it as demonstrative, suggestive, and provocative of a type of liturgical style of sacred poetry that blends contemporary literary expression with traditional theology, applying the ageless Scriptural revelation to current societal and individual needs, with the ultimate goal of confirming the relationship of the individual to God *via* Word and Sacraments.

I would like to hybridize the American product with seed from historical and contemporary foreign traditions by way of translation, just as those foreign traditions are doing by making American and British hymnody their own by rendering them in their own idioms.

PW: *What in the current hymnic scene gratifies you?*

JV: The discovery of kindred spirits with the same ideals and principles as mine, but expressed in their own styles which differ from writer to writer. To me this is imitative of the psalms composed by various authors, all of them leading the song of the church in their own voices. I am delighted to find a kinship with hymn writers such as Timothy Dudley-Smith, Erik Routley, Fred Pratt Green, Thomas Troeger, Carl Daw, Brian Wren, and to be the heir of a galaxy of writers ancient and modern, too numerous to mention, who wrote texts I wish I had written.

PW: *Is there anything which alarms you?*

JV: I have alluded to that in the paragraph about my influence. I am dismayed, if not alarmed, over the catering to the lowest common denominator of poetic and musical taste in liturgy and hymnody, instead of bringing the masses up to a higher standard and more mature level of expression in worship. Forsaking the Bible as a standard, intellectual growth is reduced to a nursery rhyme level and primitive rhythms long outgrown and abandoned by Christians serious about increasing knowledge and familiarity with the boundless wisdom and majesty and glory of God. Instead of satisfying the cry

149

for bread, more and more churches are offering circus enter-tainment and foot-stomping, hand-waving miracle shows. And this is reflected in what millions are provided as instruments of praise. What a pity that so many are never introduced to the glorious expressions of a Bach or Handel!

PW: *What do you think the future of American/English hymnody holds?*

JV: That would seem to depend on the types of liturgical and hymnic influences that express and sustain the faith of the church as they did (or did not) in the past. I would hope and pray that the explosion of hymnody of quality and relevance today bodes well for this generation of worshipers. Much will depend not only on hymnal compilers, but on the maturity and persuasiveness of local pastors and church musicians. This would suggest required seminary courses in worship, liturgy, and hymnology, and comparable church musicians' and cantors' associations. Essential too would be a serious evaluation of current popular trends in the church's song, and a critical selection of worship materials to serve the short timespan given the church in these rapidly shrinking "last days" and desperate needs.

PW: *Could you choose a couple of your texts as your favorites?*

JV: This is as difficult as saying which children one loves the most. But I would place at least two at the top of the list: "Now the Silence" and "God of the Sparrow," marking their 25th and 10th anniversaries respectively. Others might be "Go, My Children, with My Blessing," "Before the Marvel of this Night," "Amid the World's Bleak Wilderness," "Catch the Vision! Share the Glory!" "God Who Built This Wondrous Planet," "Christ Goes Before," "Lord of Lords, Adored by Angels," "Source of Breath from Time's Beginning," and of translations, "God, My Lord, My Strength" and "Now Greet the Swiftly Changing Year." Quite a number of candidates for number three!

PW: *How do you feel you have been treated by hymnal editors?*

JV: Quite well considering the first of my hymns was written when I was 49 and unable to copyright any of my texts, since my employer considered any productions as his (their) property. The largest number of texts were produced after my retirement at the age of 67. Another reason for the slow and scattered inclusion of my hymns in hymnals was my reticence in pushing or foisting my work on publishers. Practically all my hymns have been introduced on their own merit and appeal. Now I can hardly keep up with the demand for new texts and translations, and there is even less time to complete several long-standing projects.

PW: *What or who influenced you? Why do you write hymns?*

JV: In my autobiographical notes, I mention a number of influences, not all by far: the biblical poets, of course; followed by the great classical hymn writers, especially the subject of my Bachelor's/Master's thesis, George Tranovsky and the *Cithara Sanctorum,* the classic Slovak/Czech Lutheran hymnal of 1636; the honor roll of Continental and British hymn writers; and, not to be slighted, classical (and Slovak) poets, great theologians and apologists, secular dramatists, and sacred and secular composers headed by J. S. Bach; learning German in the second grade, and later, Latin, Greek, and Hebrew; studying the violin; singing in choruses; voracious reading in all fields; and professors Richard Caemmerer and Theodore Graebner, O. P. Kretzmann and Martin Franzmann, Jaroslav Pelikan and Martin Marty, etc.

Why do I write hymns? Because I am inspired to by the contemplation of the mysteries of God's plan of salvation as revealed in Jesus Christ, because I am compelled to write the kind of hymns I myself admire and like, and because I am asked to write hymns for various occasions. I would like to think my inclination toward poetry and my study and practice of the art are one way of recognizing and using a talent I have been given.

PW: *What process do you follow when writing?*

JV: After I have selected or been given a theme, I ruminate on it and fill pages of notes, many of them poetic phrases or lines. Then I settle on an appropriate poetic form (unless an extant tune has been chosen for a new text). Only a few metrical forms are out of bounds, since there are many musicians/

composers who are eager to tackle a previously unused form. Once the theology is established, I attempt to cast the theme into authentic poetry, subjecting it to ruthless criticism and revision. I hesitate to release a text that is contrived or contains clichés and overused rhymes and poetic patterns. Not all creations are the result of pure inspiration, though many, if not most, make me wonder whether I actually wrote those lines and stanzas.

PW: *Do you want to add anything?*

JV: This whole hymn writing experience has been unplanned and unexpected. I find myself driven by a compulsion to use this gift and complete related projects against a rapidly dwindling time span. The demand for hymn texts has forced me to restudy biblical and Lutheran theology, a tautological exercise, and to arrive at basic discoveries and conclusions expressed in simple terms, such as "everything is a gift of God" as a definition of grace, and gratitude as the evidence of faith and the motivation for good works, the greatest being love.

I agree with Martin Franzmann that "true theology is doxology." I believe pastors and lay theologians are best equipped to write hymns—if they are poets as well. I credit my 18 years in the full-time parish ministry as essential for writing theologically practical and applicable hymns. And I finally see how my ethnic background and interest and second-language fluency equipped me for my first literary and poetic projects: translating Slovak and Czech classic literature. For me at least, great writers provided me with an exercise in mastering literary forms, into which I could eventually pour an inspired thought or theme.

It was not until I was in my forties that I realized I have been struggling with worship all my life, before and during my pastoral ministry. The struggle forced me to examine and contend with something I had in common with all Christians, and, unconsciously, with all human beings. Both "Now the Silence" and "God of the Sparrow" grew out of that struggle. No wonder many people identify with it when I admit it openly. This is the common ground from which I begin and

JAROSLAV J. VAJDA

will write from until I reach that perfect expression of gratitude and praise befitting the glory of a gracious God.

Also, if in any way I can raise the level of wonder and
appreciation of God's awesome creation, justification, and
sanctification as it has been raised for me by the Scriptures
and by so many creative artists, I will have made some profitable use of my time and talents, although I always regret
the wasted years and opportunities for even greater growth
and closer relationship with Christ.

Christ goes before, and we are called to follow,
and all who follow find the Way, the Truth, the Life.

Where is that Way we near despaired of finding:
     the Way that comes from God and leads to God,
     the realm where God is love and love is King,
     a whole new order for a world astray!
Who wants to live where there's no love like this?
Is this the Kingdom we are ready for and desperate
     to find?
Christ goes before ...

Where is that Truth we near despaired of knowing:
     the Truth that comes from God and leads to God,
     the power to set us free, the power to change,
     that faces Pilate and the cross and wins?
Who wants to live where there's no peace like this?
Is this the Power we are ready for and desperate
     to know?
Christ goes before ...

Where is that Life we near despaired of having:
     the Life that comes from God and leads to God,
     the hope of glory only Christ can give,
     that shatters death and grief with Easter joy?
Who wants to live where there's no joy like this?
Is this the Glory we are ready for and desperate
     to have?
Christ goes before ...

CHAPTER 11

Brian A. Wren

I come with joy to be with God,
    forgiven, loved and free,
the life of Jesus to recall,
    in love laid down for me.

I come with Christians far and near
    to find, as all are fed,
the new community of love
    in Christ's communion bread.

As Christ breaks bread, and bids us share,
    each proud division ends.
The love that made us, makes us one,
    and strangers now are friends.

And thus we meet, and better know
    the Presence, ever near,
and join our hearts, and sing with joy
    that Christ is risen here.

Together met, together bound,
    together we will pray,
then go with joy to meet the world
    and live the Jesus Way.

Biographical Sketch

Brian Wren was born in 1936 in Romford, Essex, England, where he attended the Royal Liberty Grammar School. He grew up during World War II, and his earliest memories are of air raid sirens, bombs, and anti-aircraft weapons. His father was in the army and spent seven years of Brian's early life away from home. Brian himself served two years in compulsory army service.

At the age of 14 Wren began attending Upminster Congregational Church in Essex, England. He was baptized there on confession of faith at the age of 19, and felt called to full-time Christian service. After he completed a Bachelor of Arts honors degree in
modern languages in 1960 at New College, Oxford, he pursued
theological study and graduated with honors in Theology from
Mansfeld College, Oxford, in 1962. Ordained in the Congregational
Church of England and Wales (now part of the United Reformed
Church in Great Britain) in 1965, he then served for five years as
pastor of Hockley and Hawkwell Congregational Church, a 110-
member congregation in suburban Essex.

During this time he completed a doctorate in theology which he
received from Oxford University in 1968. His thesis was on the Language of Prophetic Eschatology in the Old Testament. He also wrote
hymns for his congregation, though his first hymn had already been
written in 1961 under the guidance of Erik Routley.

From 1970 to 1975 Wren was adult education consultant to the
Churches Committee on World Development. This was a joint committee of the British Council of Churches and the British Catholic
Mission and Justice and Peace Commissions for England and Wales.
Following that, from 1976 to 1983, he served as coordinator and
team member of Third World First, a student-based world poverty
campaign. He was also Council Chair and Executive Board member of the charity, War and Want. The concerns these groups represent are a clue to Brian Wren's passions and have not been lost
in his hymn writing.

Since 1983 Wren has been what he describes as a "freelance
minister." Without a regular salary, he relies on writing and workshops for support. Churches and seminaries sponsor the workshops
which usually concern worship, faith, hymnody, and issues related
to gender. The last matter, gender, has led Wren to concerns about
language—which he addresses at workshops and evidences in his
hymn writing.

In the early 1980s Hope Publishing Company published Brian
Wren's texts in North America and invited him for a summer tour.
From this first visit, in 1983, many other invitations followed. On a
summer visit to Denver in 1986, he met Susan Heafield, an ordained
minister in the United Methodist Church. Acquaintance grew into

friendship. Much later in both their life stories, in August of 1991, they were married in Vestal, New York, and now live in Topsham, Maine. Susan is Associate Pastor at Brunswick United Methodist Church. From their former marriages Susan has one son Nathan in his mid-teens, and Brian has a daughter Hilary and son Nicholas, both in their mid-twenties.

The author of more than 150 hymns which have been included in many hymnals, Wren has also written two books, *Education for Justice* and *What Language Shall I Borrow?* Both relate to and express his ethical concerns for justice. He was a member of the committee which prepared *New Church Praise,* a hymn supplement produced in 1975 when the Congregational and Presbyterian churches in the United Kingdom joined to form the United Reformed Church.

Publications

Brian Wren's Hymn Texts, 1963–1985: A Guide for Composers and Hymnal Editors. n. p.

Bring Many Names: 35 New Hymns by Brian Wren. Carol Stream: Hope Publishing Company, 1989.

Education for Justice. New York: Orbis, 1977.

Faith Looking Forward: The Hymns & Songs of Brian Wren with many Tunes by Peter Cutts. Carol Stream: Hope Publishing Company, 1983.

Mainly Hymns. Manchester: John Paul the Preacher's Press, 1980.

New Beginnings: 30 New Hymns for the 90's. Carol Stream: Hope Publishing Company, 1992.

Praising a Mystery: 30 New Hymns by Brian Wren. Carol Stream: Hope Publishing Company, 1986.

What Language Shall I Borrow?—God-Talk in Worship: A Male Response to Feminist Theology. New York: Crossroad, 1989.

Numerous articles, education packs, worship materials, and multimedia productions.

Hymns

A body, broken, on a cross
A child, a woman and a man
A dancer's body leaps and falls
A man of ancient time and place
A mountain rises
A prophet-woman broke a jar
A stranger, knocking on a door
A woman in a world of men
A woman in the crowd
Acclaim with jubilation
All-perceiving lover
All saints
Are you the friendly God?
Arise, shine out, your light has come
As man and woman
At the table of the world

Born into love
Bring many names
By purpose and by chance
By contact with the crucified

Can a man be kind and caring
Child, when Herod wakes
Christ crucified now is alive
Christ is alive!
Christ is risen! Shout hosanna!
Christ loves the church
Christ upon the mountain peak
Christ will come again
Come, build the church
Come, celebrate the call of God
Come, holy breath
Come, let us love

Daughter, Mary, saying yes
Dear Sister God

Deep in the shadows of the past
Doom and danger Jesus knows
Dust and ashes touch our face

Each seeking faith
Eternal wisdom, timely friend
Ever-journeying friend

Faith looking forward
For the bread

Give thanks for music-making art
Go forth in faith
Go now in peace
God is one, unique and holy
God, give us freedom to lament
God of Jeremiah
God of many names
God remembers
God, the All-Holy
Good is the flesh
Great lover, calling us to share
Great soaring spirit
Grief of ending, wordless sorrow

Hail, undiminished love
Her baby, newly breathing
Here am I
Here and now, if you love
Here and now, in your need
Here hangs a man discarded
Holy Spirit, hear us as we pray
Holy Spirit, storm of love
Holy weaver, deftly intertwining
How can we name a love?
How good to thank our God
How great the mystery of faith
How shall I sing to God?

WITH TONGUES OF FIRE

How wonderful the Three-in-One

I am going to Calvary
I am worthy, full of worth!
I come with joy
I have no bucket, and the well is deep
I'll try, my love, to love you
I love this land
If I could visit Bethlehem?
In water we grow
In great Calcutta Christ is known
Is this a day of new beginnings

Jesus comes today
Jesus is good news to all the poor
Jesus is with God
Joyful is the dark

Let all creation dance
Let hope and sorrow now unite
Life is great!
Look back and see the apostles' road
Lord Christ, the Father's mighty son
Lord God, your love has called us here
Lord Jesus, if I love and serve my neighbor
Lord, let me welcome timely death
Lord, thank you for the Jews
Lord, when you came to Jordan
Love alone unites us
Love is the only hope
Love makes a bridge

May the sending one sing in you

Name unnamed
Not only acts of evil will

O how joyfully!

Once from a European shore

Peace is a song
Praise God for the harvest
Praise God, from whom all blessings flow
Praise God, the giver and the gift
Praise the God who changes places
Praise the lover of creation
Praise to the maker
Prophets give us hope

Sing my song backwards
Sing praises old and new
Stand up, friends!

Thanks you, God, for water, soil and air
The gifts of God
The gospel spoke with foreign tongue
The horrors of our century
The light of God is shining bright
The waiting night
There's a spirit in the air
This is a story full of love
This we can do
Traveling, traveling over the world
Tree of fire
True friends

Water in the snow
We are not our own
We are your people
We bring, you take
We offer Christ
We plough and sow
We want to care
Weep for the dead
Welcome the wild one
When a baby in your arms

When all is ended
When Christ was lifted up from the earth
When God is a child
When grief is raw
When I have failed
When joy is drowned
When love is found
When minds and bodies meet as one
When on life a darkness falls
When pain and terror strike by chance
Who comes?
Who is God?
Who is She?
Will God be judge?
Will you come and see the light?
With humble justice clad and crowned
Woman in the night
Wonder of wonders

You were a child of mine

Interview

PW: Can you summarize your personal theology?
BW: My theology is in what I write. One day I may write it up
more systematically, but I don't have time at present. I think
I've been enabled to articulate some fresh, and some new,
theological insights in hymn-poems, but that's for others to
evaluate. Some labels I and others have pinned on me are:
Arminian, Calvinist without the "TULIP" (*T*otal depravity,
*U*nconditional election, *L*imited atonement, *I*rresistible grace,
*P*erseverance of the saints); Feminist; white male listening to
feminist, womanist, Asian, African, African-American and
other critical theologies; Reformed; Congregationalist (in the
English, Dissenting sense); Niebuhrian; not Barthian; a high
view of scripture and a low view of fundamentalism; trinitarian, based on experience and conviction, not tying trinitarian
theology to traditional language; eclectic, suspicious of sys-

tems; believing in no castle of immunity from sin, or infallibility, but believing also in God's grace to transform and renew.

PW: *What do you wish you had written (and presumably still may)?*

BW: There is still much to be done, but I only know the next thing to be written. So I can't really answer this question.

PW: *Are there any of your hymns you now wish you had not written?*

BW: There are some *things* I wish I had not done, but I can't think of any *hymns* I wish I hadn't written. Several I've had to revise; some are attempts that don't work, for varied or technical reasons; some get dated (such as "Life Is Great" in *Faith Looking Forward*).

PW: *How do you see the hymn functioning in worship?*

BW: Briefly, I understand a hymn to be a poem of faith, sung by a group of people in a particular time and place. That's a snapshot definition: it includes important elements, but doesn't claim to cover the entire landscape. Good hymn song is corporate (bringing us together as the body of Christ), corporeal (we who are paleface Western Christians use our God-given bodies more fully in singing than elsewhere in our body-distrusting traditions of worship and theology), credal (expressing our faith, hope, yearning, theology, etc., in the presence of God), contemporary (not "about" but "from" the reality of the world in which we live) and hopefully beautiful in melody and lyrics.

PW: *How do you perceive your influence? Is it regional or more broad than that?*

BW: It's restricted to the English-speaking world, more in North America than elsewhere. In the very small world of hymnody, and on a modest scale, it's international.

PW: *How do you see your work in relation to late 20th-century hymnody generally?*

BW: I'm in the Anglo-Saxon tradition, which tries to combine theological freshness and depth with simple language, to express people's theology, and at times stretch or re-articulate it. Other traditions include the (white) gospel song, African-American hymnody, praise music and scripture songs, and the quite varied styles becoming available to us from South America, Africa, and Asia. Recently I've been able to expand into the less formal world of the song lyric, which I enjoy.

PW: *What in the current hymnic scene gratifies you?*
BW: The emergence of new writers in North America, several of whom are being published in my newsletter, *NewSong*.

PW: *What in the current scene alarms you?*
BW: Triviality in the church; the long-standing American confusion between the flag and the cross; racism, sexism, heterosexism, so little understood, so little repented by our churches; abuses of power, in families and in the church, by powerful people (usually men) and nations; the exponential increase in world hunger, the scale of poverty and homelessness in Britain and the United States; authoritarian use of the Bible as a cudgel and rule book; denominational insularity, national insularity; uncritical acceptance of our economic order as "necessary," "natural," or "Christian."

PW: *What does the future of American/English hymnody hold?*
BW: I don't know.

PW: *What do you regard as the three (or two or one) most representative hymns you have written?*
BW: I can think of two or three that seem to have become (in a minor way) "classic," and 20 or so that seem to have made a mark, but beyond that it's difficult to say. My most frequently published hymn is probably "I Come with Joy to Meet My Lord," followed by "Christ Is Alive" and "There's a Spirit in the Air."

PW: *How do you feel you have been treated by hymnal editors?*
BW: Pretty well, generally. I edit my own words, so the question really relates to tunes. Most hymnal editors take their task seriously, and deal faithfully. Most annoying are those who don't set up systems to consult authors about possible changes, but make clumsy unauthorized alterations that reach the

author at proof stage. I refrain from mentioning names, but the United Methodists *didn't* act that way.

PW: *What or who influenced you? Why do you write hymns?*
BW: Isaac Watts; Erik Routley; Fred Kaan; Thomas Troeger; the theologians mentioned in my answer to "theological accents"; George Caird, my tutor and doctoral supervisor; those named in the notes and introductions to my hymns collections; my mother, father, spouse, children; etc.

PW: *What process do you follow when writing?*
BW: Sometimes I begin with an existing tune, and let it suggest a mood, themes, phrases. Sometimes I carefully plan and research the themes I want to express, then wait for images, phrases, and rhymes. Sometimes I am "given" rhymes, first lines, phrases, which I write down, then work to develop. Hymn writing is not a mystical elite experience, done in a crackle of laser-light from above. Like any problem-solving activity it includes planning, research, thinking, waiting for "inspiration," then working again to shape and develop what has been "given."

PW: *Do you want to add anything?*
BW: In the early 1980s I emerged from a period of questioning about worship and the church to believe again in the value and power of Sunday worship (the liturgy) as the church's indispensable self-defining focus, whereby we are formed in faith as we give glory to God and seek to be found by the One who encounters us. As one of my hymns puts it, worship calls for "the best that we can do and say; the utmost care of skill and art," so I am frustrated when churches settle for less than that. Yet when that is done, the focus is not art, but God, because our best endeavors are "sweepers of the Spirit's way / to reach the depths of every heart" ("How Great the Mystery of Faith," No. 22 in *Bring Many Names*).

WITH TONGUES OF FIRE

Christ is alive! Let Christians sing.
    His cross stands empty to the sky.
Let streets and homes with praises ring.
    His love in death shall never die.

Christ is alive! No longer bound
    to distant years in Palestine
he comes to claim the here and now
    and conquer every place and time.

Not throned above, remotely high,
    untouched, unmoved by human pains
but daily, in the midst of life,
    our Savior with the Father reigns.

In every insult, rift, and war
    where color, scorn, or wealth divide,
he suffers still, yet loves the more,
    and lives, though ever crucified.

Christ is alive! His Spirit burns
    through this and every future age,
till all creation lives and learns
    his joy, his justice, love and praise.

CHAPTER 12

A Round-table Discussion

The publisher suggested that one of the sections of this book be a round-table discussion by "people in the know about late 20th-century hymnody." (I shall attempt a more personal appraisal in the closing chapter.) Together we compiled a list of persons who had expertise in some aspect—often many aspects—of hymnody and who had thought about the "current state of the art."

I asked each of these to respond briefly to two of the questions the hymn writers themselves had been asked and add any other salient concerns. The questions were "What in the current hymnic scene gratifies you?" and "What in the current scene alarms you?" The 11 people who responded voiced many common themes, with a rich and wide variety of related concerns. I edited their responses into the following discussion which they had the chance to re-edit. It has the character of conversation, not careful logical progression. That may be a liability, but it does match the interrelated complexity of the issues we face. And, if it seems to end abruptly without closure, that also reflects the reality.

First, let me identify the participants. They are an impressive group with complementary expertise.

Hedda Durnbaugh, Librarian, Juniata College, Huntingdon, Pennsylvania—author, translator, bibliographer

C. Michael Hawn, Associate Professor of Sacred Music, Southern Methodist University, Dallas, Texas—church musician, author, teacher

Madeleine Marshall, Professor of English, University of San Diego, San Diego, California—author, translator, teacher

David W. Music, Associate Professor of Church Music, Southwestern Baptist Theological Seminary, Fort Worth, Texas—church musician, author, teacher, editor of *The Hymn*

Susan Palo Cherwien, Minneapolis, Minnesota—singer, musician, poet, teacher, hymnist

Gail Ramshaw, Associate Professor of Religion, LaSalle University, Philadelphia—author, scholar of liturgical language, teacher

Paul A. Richardson, Professor of Church Music, The Southern Baptist Theological Seminary, Louisville, Kentucky—church musician, author, editor, teacher, president of The Hymn Society in the United States and Canada

Carl Schalk, Distinguished Professor of Music Emeritus, Concordia University, River Forest, Illinois—church musician, composer, author, editor, teacher

W. Thomas Smith, Fort Worth, Texas—church musician, executive director of The Hymn Society in the United States and Canada

Vernon Wicker, Professor of Music, Seattle Pacific University, Seattle, Washington—author, translator, singer, editor of the *Hymnology Annual: an International Forum on the Hymn and Worship*

Russell Schulz-Widmar, Professor of Music, The Episcopal Seminary of the Southwest, Austin, Texas—church musician, author, teacher, hymnal editor, past president of The Hymn Society in the United States and Canada

PW: *When I pose the questions "What in the current scene gratifies you?" and "What in the current scene alarms you?" you all appear to agree that both the amount and the variety of the hymn writing we are experiencing is gratifying.*

Music: There is a remarkable diversity of quality from which to choose. New hymns are being written at an incredible rate. They are finding their way quickly into the services of the church. Much fine material is being resurrected from the past by hymnologists. A "world hymnody" is rapidly developing, as more and more texts and tunes from Third World countries and ethnic groups find their way into Western hymnals. The number of congregational "song styles" that are considered to be "appropriate" for worship has expanded dramatically.

Wicker: It is exciting to experience the output of excellent British and American hymns (texts and music) during the past decades. We have come to the point where there is no longer an excuse *not* to gather contemporary materials of consistently outstanding quality for new hymnals. Whether editing a hymnal or choosing hymns for next Sunday's service, we can now select substantial works of enduring quality from the ancient past as well as current times, both those that make classic statements of doctrine and those that effectively address contemporary issues without sacrificing literary and theological quality and integrity.

I am grateful that the much-talked-about globalization in hymnody is moving forward through the fine practical and scholarly work of people such as I-to Loh (*Sound the Bamboo*), David Graber (*The Cheyenne Hymnal*), Pablo Sosa (*Todas Las Voces*), Howard Olson (*African Hymns*), et al.

Hawn: The diversity of hymn literature found in hymnbooks published since 1975 is gratifying. I would add the following to flesh that out: intentional relating of hymn texts to Scripture, especially canticle and psalm paraphrases; more use of global hymnody, i.e., hymnody outside the Euro-American sphere; limited, but growing introduction of other congregational song forms beyond standard hymns in stanzas, such as Taizé materials and other shorter, repetitive congregational songs; more use of refrains (or antiphons) as a hymn form, not allowing this form to be almost exclusively the domain of gospel song and its offspring; more use of inclusive language (both for God and humanity) that is integral to the hymn rather than superimposed following the original writing; more hymns on the human condition, e.g., hunger, conflict, use of natural resources, racism, etc.; more African-American materials in current hymnals; varied approaches to singing the psalms.

Richardson: The availability of excellent new texts is the strongest aspect of the current scene in hymnody. Many of these texts are rich with biblical quotation, paraphrase, and allusion—something that was largely missing from the first wave of the "hymn explosion." The formulation of new resources for singing psalms and other poetic biblical expressions is a great asset for the church. In addition, there are splendid new texts that both permit and require the church to address significant questions related to the church's worship and witness, as well as those that provide appropriate ways (both in language and theology) to praise and to respond to God in the late 20th century. Among the various writers, there is a broad variety of styles of expression, with high poetic quality in many of these.

PW: Tom, your perspective at the Hymn Society has made it possible for you to watch hymnic developments over a number of years from a widely ecumenical perspective.

Smith: The easiest response to your questions is to dwell on the negative. However, I am very encouraged by the many positive aspects in congregational song of the last decade of the 20th century.

As many as 35 denominational and commercial hymnals have been produced in the United States during the last 15 years. That is a positive sign that congregational song is alive and well.

The repertory is being influenced by the cultural and ethnic diversity in the United States, as well as from around the world. That is a positive influence.

The large number of first-rate hymn words and music writers continue to provide worshipers with new insights into the faith. That provides positive faith growth.

PW: You also are wont to focus on the uniqueness of hymn singing.

Smith: The only place where unrehearsed communal singing happens is in worship. An estimated 60 million people in the United States worship on any given weekend. That many are exposed to and participate in singing the congregational song.

PW: Hymns are not without their power!

Schalk: A good hymn—both words and music—expands our horizons, moving us beyond what we think we are capable of, and helping us to achieve what we never thought we could. Examples of hymns which do this can be found both in the tradition of the church's hymnody and in the new songs of our time. To discern these and distinguish them from the trendy and faddish aspects of our day—whether texts or tunes—makes the 20th century an exciting time in which to live, work, and make music to the Lord.

PW: *That suggests there are some problems. While all of you appear to agree with the richness among us, you also express some concerns as well. Can we isolate some of those?*

Schalk: Before we do that, there is another gratifying aspect of the current scene that should be identified—the number of congregations which are commissioning new texts and new tunes for use in their churches. While this may or may not bring forth any new hymnic gems, it reflects an attitude on the part of many in those congregations that new hymnody can be a lively contribution to the parish worship life.

Cherwien: There is cause for hope in late 20th-century hymnody! Many neglected or forgotten themes of Christian theology and life have been picked up by courageous and skilled poets and shaped into ennobling art. I think, as an example, of Brian Wren's provocative "Good is the flesh," which embodies some of the startling implications of the incarnation as no prior text I can recall. And Jaroslav Vajda's "God of the Sparrow," a poignant reflection on creation from an unusual vantage point. Such texts pull us out of our parochial concerns and offer us a broadened experience of life touched by the Divine. Such is the power of art.

Marshall: Perhaps the best news about 20th-century hymnody is its return of hymn poetry to the common speech of ordinary people—this after the Victorian wandering about in the linguistic wilderness of pseudokingjamesese. The language of our best modern hymns is as perfectly easy, as transparent, as the language of Paul Gerhardt and Isaac Watts.

The bad news—not exactly the effect of this cause—is the excruciating banality, the hopeless flatness of all too many hymns. Perhaps the archaic language reminded earlier hymnwriters of the expectations of the tradition. Perhaps the demands of writing in an older version of English kept the hopelessly inept from penning hymns. Perhaps the biblical resonance of archaic language enforced the accountability of the hymn texts, signaling writer and singer alike that "this had better be important." We lost something with the silly old language.

PW: *Gail, I sense you share and don't share this concern—or want to say some different things about it.*

Ramshaw: My greatest concern in the area of hymnody is that, while repeated singing of the great hymns of the tradition can be, and has been for many Christians, one of the most significant vehicles for the formation of spirituality, many of the masterpieces of Christian hymnody are so seriously flawed by androcentric language, imagery, and assumptions that their continued use must be questioned. When does a hymn text function as poetry, its vintage improving its power, and when does archaic metaphor weaken the faith with its absurdities? Our difficulty with this issue leads to everyone who has passed freshman English trying to write new hymns, in which the heresy is matched only by the sheer insipidity of the lines.

Richardson: My greatest concern about the present situation is the relative ineffectiveness in making a vital connection between the excellent resources we have and the lives of the majority of those in the pews. This problem has many causes, I suspect.

The fault lies partly with congregational and denominational leaders who have largely failed to make evident the practical value of new hymns. This failure occurs principally in selecting and enabling the use of the materials. (By enabling, I mean the creation of a climate for successful participation through such means as indirect education, direct teaching, and effective leadership from the organist/song leader/cantor.)

There is weak leadership from pastors who have not grasped the real importance of congregational song and who have but passing acquaintance with their own hymnals—let alone the rich resources of historic or contemporary hymnody. This can be traced, in large measure, to their training.

To be fair, there is also weak "followship," which is but one evidence of lethargy in churches—lethargy bred by a society that prizes passivity and entertainment over participation and stewardship. This attitude is inadequately confronted by church leaders, clergy and laity, who have not grasped the tasks of the church as leader and interpreter, but have abdicated the priestly and prophetic roles to the "apparently powerful," that amorphous body of consumers herded by commercial interests.

PW: Vernon, you would agree, I think.

Wicker: It is frustrating and alarming, puzzling and sometimes annoying, that so many church leaders, pastors, worship leaders and musicians from practically every church and denominational group glibly accept the alleged fact that there are only "*old* hymns and *new* songs" and that no other options exist. They are uninformed about the vast repertoire of genuinely new, high quality hymns—hymns that would better meet at least part of their congregational singing needs than so much of the theologically poor, musically shallow repertoire of commercialism sung in so many churches today.

Hawn: I perceive that hymnal editors and committees are often doing their work in vain. I am not sure that the flood of new English language hymnals published in the United States since 1975 is having an impact on congregational singing. Without pastors and musicians willing to use these materials, they will have little impact.

I would add a few other concerns. 1) We need singable tunes for new texts. There are many tunes available, but there is no successor to Ralph Vaughan Williams. 2) We need more of substance that speaks to young people and children. 3) We need more hymnody that speaks of science in post-Copernican terms. 4) Particularly alarming is the replacement of traditional standard (pre-20th century) hymnody with choruses (or "hymnlets" as Don Hustad calls them). 5) With much theology and preaching seeking to reach the lowest common denominator, I worry that hymns of theological substance and

173

poetic integrity do not often have a context in which to be fairly heard.

PW: *Gail, you probably want to voice a warning about singing only new hymns.*

Ramshaw: Our singing too high a percentage of new hymns eliminates one of the purposes of hymn singing: to bind us to the masterpieces of the tradition, to connect our old age with our childhood.

Schalk: The tremendous amount of hymn writing activity can be a two-edged sword. Any congregation can only absorb so much hymnody—and it is usually less than we think—and still keep alive a solid core of congregational repertoire. In a hundred years or so there probably will be only a few of the many highly touted "new hymns" currently in use which will have made it past our own time and into the more permanent repertoire of the church.

PW: *That raises the question of quality, a concern many of you expressed.*

Richardson: If there is a fault in the materials themselves, I am inclined to lay it at the feet of the composers and editors rather than the authors. While there are many fine new tunes and numerous creative matches, we have not discovered the mix of musical languages (and we must cultivate multilingual musicality for a number of reasons) that will help worshipers to engage the text with confidence and enthusiasm.

Schulz-Widmar: Too many mediocre biblical versifications have been published in recent hymnals. It seems that a lower standard is brought into play when a hymn is a biblical versification. This does no favors to the congregation or the Bible.

Cherwien: There is a lack of fear and trembling. The sense of awe and responsibility which should infuse the hymnic process seems missing from much of what is written at this time. No humility, no repentance, no cross (in one hymn supplement of over two hundred hymns, I found only five references to the cross, not one to repentance), no transcendence, no mystery. This is evidenced not only by the tenor of the texts and such devices as having the congregation speak for God, but also in the generally poor craft and quality of the writing. The Creator of our existence deserves the finest and truest we can create.

PW: Hedda, I take it you would agree, but add your own twist.

Durnbaugh: I have a concern in addition to the deplorable surfeit of shallow texts and tunes on the current hymn market. This concern pertains to the continued neglect of the hymnal as a resource for private devotions. Probably as a reaction to the often misunderstood so-called subjective hymnody of earlier eras and cheap 19th-century hymnody, the trend in this half century has rather consistently been toward emphasis of community and production of topical and programmatic hymn texts. Sunday morning worship continues to be seen as the primary use of most American hymnals. The music is almost exclusively "upbeat" and in major keys. The spirituality of a congregation at worship is usually measured by the tempo of the music and the volume of the sound.

Schalk: In past centuries, much hymnody was written for private devotional purposes and found a comfortable home in that context. Today, budding text and tune writers expect that their latest opus must immediately be heard in corporate worship, whether or not it is really suitable for that purpose. This expectation exists largely because we have, over the centuries, blurred the distinction between hymnody which is more appropriate for corporate worship and that which is more appropriate for private, personal devotional use.

Smith: While we should be concerned about the decline in quality of much that is being written, we should remember that throughout the history of congregational singing there have been peripheral expressions. These may have served as temporary expressions but have since disappeared.

PW: Tom sent me an article by Timothy Sharp on the loss of mystery. It parallels the concern Susan expressed. Hedda, you seem to have similar thoughts about quality and our age being short on repentance and mystery.

Durnbaugh: In examining the topical indexes of current hymnals of major denominations, one notices an absence of entries dealing with the shadow- or down-side of life. Instead of "Doubt" one finds only "Faith"; instead of "Grief," only "Consolation"; instead of "Loss," "Hope." The list could be extended. It is small wonder that many Christians who want to turn to hymns in times of inner and outer distress have their spiritual needs met only by the spiritual pap that is produced so glibly and prolifically today.

This situation has as much to do with the nature of American churches as with their hymnodies. In this country, churchly and secular rationalism has never experienced a counter-movement other than the somewhat looked-down-upon revivals of the 19th and 20th centuries. Where congregations believe in their ability to improve and better themselves and the world around them, the shadow-sides of life are their taboos. If a certain lack of spirituality is felt, seminars and workshops are offered to cover this gap as if spirituality could be learned in a few easy lessons (just as hymn writing). As long as hymns of universal spiritual value but of non-programmatic or topical nature are not seen to have value and are therefore kept out of the hymnals, the mystery of the faith and the numinous will continue to escape us, and Christians seeking the right words for their troubled conditions will look in vain to the hymnal for help.

PW: Some of you also see diversity as a mixed blessing.

Music: All the diversity is a plus, but there is often a negative side to it as well. For a long time, there has been a sort of hymnic *lingua franca*—a body of hymns common to most American Christians. This commonality seems to be breaking down at a tremendous rate, so that one can no longer assume that "everyone knows" this or that hymn. A lot is gained by having so many choices, but a great deal is also being lost.

PW: Madeleine, you seem to extend the problem to "spiritual colonialism."

Marshall: The news of an international world bursting with Christian song is good. Modern English-speaking academic hymnologists are *not* in charge of the songs of believers after all. It's great that we can acknowledge the rich diversity of song, representing everything we can think of in our modern hymnals. This keeps us righteously modest and reminds us of current events. The bad news is that these songs are often poorly selected, inexpertly translated, and misused in worship. This suggests an alarming misunderstanding of the purpose and function of hymns. As an approved formulation of common pious sentiment, hymnody is culturally specific. When, through song, we lay claim to the piety or experience of other people we engage in a terrible sort of spiritual colonialism.

PW: Vernon, I think you have a bit different perspective.

Wicker: Regarding the globalization of congregational singing, I worry that people seem content to let this process merely be a minor concern of a few Sunday schoolteachers for elementary ages as they sing a little song from somewhere else, thereby missing the opportunity to learn important, substantial articulations of the faith in different ways from our own. It also seems that many of our leaders and congregations are unwilling to make the necessary effort to broaden horizons. Through international travel and communications the world *is* getting smaller. If our churches neither make an honest gesture toward other cultures nor learn from them, we will have missed fulfilling at least part of the "Great Commission." It is through carefully selected hymnody that we can avoid the pitfall.

PW: Russell, I take it you want to affirm the "folk's song," but you also want to affirm the value of editorial expertise.

Schulz-Widmar: Denominations expect their hymnal editors to react to the rank and file faithful. This is of course entirely appropriate and necessary. But it seems that some hymnals have been put together almost entirely by popular vote; too many pages are given over to the "golden goldies" and the recent "hits" and not enough pages are given over to the "new literature" or hymns that are potentially valuable but are new and therefore unknown to the rank and file. Good hymnal editors will have expertise in generally unfamiliar hymns— both old and new—and predicting potential future use. This expertise should be trusted.

PW: You push this a bit farther, don't you, to concerns about political correctness?

Schulz-Widmar: I'm concerned about the extent to which the editing of hymnals has become politicized. As an essentially folk-loric art form that has evolved over centuries, hymnody cannot be made entirely "politically correct." Hymnody is simply too sprawling and varied. A lot of good work has been done in the areas of modernization and correction, but I mourn seeing a great hymn rejected or made ugly (and ultimately useless in liturgy therefore) when a phrase or word is viewed as incorrect. The editing of hymns ultimately must be in the hands of artists, not in the hands of politicians or lawyers.

PW: And you're also concerned about page layout in our hymnals, right?

Schulz-Widmar: The practice seen in a number of recent hymnals—that of gathering very brief descriptions of the hymns at the bottoms of pages, almost like footnotes—needs to be reevaluated. A hymnal should be rich, various, and interesting, a living bequest and repository of all sorts of things suitable for congregational singing. These qualities are made clearer to the book's users by accurate, prominent descriptions of the hymns. The footnote format suggests sameness, namelessness, disconnectedness; it suggests uniformity when in fact variety characterizes us and our literature. We read from the top of a page to the bottom. Therefore, good, accurate, interesting descriptions should be printed above the hymn.

PW: *Madeleine, you probably want to return to Russell's earlier point about "political correctness."*

Marshall: Inclusivity marks a genuine commitment to hymnody as a means of educating believers. To the extent that the Christian faith in the 20th century is incompatible with racism, sexism, and classism, this sensitivity belongs on our hymn agenda.

The bad news is that good hymns demand more than good intentions. This new political agenda is problematic to the extent to which "consciousness-raising," the confrontational 20th-century model for education as liberation, is practiced with language. The battle is fought with words. Forced into consciousness through language, we are conditioned to flinch at black and white, dark and light, father, brother, and king above. Words are good or bad according to a standard, an authority, that has nothing to do with common sense or metaphorical exactness. However useful for heightening awareness, attitude correction through vocabulary control is doomed to fail. However we attempt to shape opinion and feeling by manipulating words, word meaning will soon conform to the attitudes, however sinful, of those who use them. Words work like that. Language changes. Pious talk and piety are not the same thing.

PW: *Susan, you also have concerns about language.*

Cherwien: There are present trends in hymn text writing that we employ to our detriment. They are tied to the "lack of fear and trembling" and born of the audacity to write without training, practice, or the discipline that an encounter with ultimate truth should inspire in us. One is the *cliché bombe*. This method is a danger for both traditional hymnists and rock-pop writer/composers. Formula: string together a group of favorite theological phrases or Scripture verses, add a congregational refrain, and the result is a forgettable text that robs the individual images of their *potentia* and washes over the congregation like a lukewarm shower. Pleasant and nonthreatening, also nontransformative and impotent.

Another trend is simply faulty technique that results in *logicide,* the killing of words. Part of the poet's craft is the art of expressing truth in new ways, of using image, story, synonym, and circumlocution to newly clothe the old. Part of what is absent in many contemporary texts is this skill. As a result, words such as "compassion," "justice," and "love" are being killed, muted, made into clichés, by overuse, from lack of craft.

PW: Theological concerns, or their absence, are imbedded in this.

Schalk: The chief concern among many is that hymnody be "contemporary"—which is usually defined as, depending upon the source, certain kinds of language used or omitted, certain subject matter favored (often dealing with various social reforms), striking new imagery, or particular kinds of musical styles or forms. These tend to be the criteria. If new hymns fill them, they are good; if they don't, they are bad. In all of this there is often an obliviousness to, a disinterest in, or lack of sensitivity to a new hymn's theology. The result is too often texts which speak a questionable theology at best, and, at worst, a theology foreign to the Christian faith.

PW: Carl, I think you have a couple other concerns.

Schalk: There is in full flower a trend which sees contemporary hymnody as a business to be exploited. The amassing of copyrights and their control becomes important. One is reminded of a similar situation in the late 1800s in connection with Gospel Song.

Another, more important, danger is that with all the emphasis on new hymnody, congregations can easily neglect the preservation and use of that body of hymnody from the church's tradition which has nourished the faith for countless generations. If we sing only new hymnody, we can easily cut ourselves off from the tradition of the church's song which provides a necessary balance and equilibrium which is sometimes lacking in congregations or among pastors and musicians obsessed only with the new.

A ROUND-TABLE DISCUSSION

PW: *Your point is similar to the one David Music and Gail Ramshaw made earlier. On another topic, does anyone share my concern that all but one of the hymn writers in this book are white males?*

Ramshaw: I am surprised that men are still dominating the field.

Marshall: Authorized poetry (approved, edited, published by a hymnal committee) is an elite idiom. Not surprisingly, *canonical* 20th-century hymnwriters are theologically educated white males. The great hymns of our day come out of experience, not theory. Their authors trust language and metaphor. They trust language—careful, precise language—to communicate and singers to understand. They insist on tangibility and defy abstraction. They build upon traditional expectations and understandings. Our best radical minds, meanwhile, are busy criticizing traditional misconceptions or rewriting history or campaigning for change. They distrust theological education, authority, and language itself.

Ramshaw: My fiercest rage is directed at the "I am God" hymn texts, my deepest sorrow with the "God is my buddy" texts, my greatest boredom with the texts which are group self-identity exercises rather than praise of God.

Marshall: Often I worry that elite, expert distrust of common believers will ruin the hymnic enterprise; that language will buckle and sink into chaos under its political burden; that banality will pass for beauty, vague ideas for profundity, sincerity for truth. When I am cheerful, I hope this crisis will pass and a new day will dawn. Then true poetry, the best contemporary piety, and a real understanding of how hymns work will produce a new world of clear, useful hymn texts.

CHAPTER 13

Some Concluding Observations

The "Hymn Explosion"

Though they are among the most significant ones, the writers in this book are not the only English-speaking hymn writers at the end of the 20th century; nor is English the only language in which hymn writing is being pursued. We do indeed live in the midst of what has aptly been called a "hymn explosion." To grasp the size of this "explosion," one has only to consider the number of texts listed here as a portion of a larger whole which is continually increasing.

The Hymns Themselves

Beyond this obvious renewal of hymnody, there are some instructive recurring themes in these pages. One is the quality of the hymns themselves. Readers probably will not agree about the precise quality of all the texts which have been listed in this book, nor will they think the capabilities of the writers are comparable. We all are likely to have our own hunches about which specific texts are of lasting value and which writers have made the most valuable contributions to the hymnic repertoire of the church. But, as a whole, the texts given here are substantial ones, not superficial, and worthy of the church's consideration.

Second, the quality of the hymns is high in part because of the labor the writers have exerted on them. It is clear that the writers interviewed here have taken hymn writing very seriously and have worked hard at it. From the many drafts of Fred Pratt Green to the concerns for structure and form of Sylvia Dunstan to the spiritual discipline of Thomas Troeger to the painstaking care of Timothy Dudley-Smith or Jaroslav Vajda, it is obvious that great effort has been expended by these writers. Though they may have written many hymns, these have not been ground out in some sort of endless and effortless profusion, but have been invested with time, effort, and relentlessly loving care.

Third, the quality is also high because of the background and preparation of the writers. In some respects their backgrounds and preparations are quite different: they come from different continents, received different training in different schools, represent different denominations and confessional positions, and are from different generations. Yet in varying though always clear and strong ways these characteristics unite them.

i) They exhibit an immersion in and knowledge of the biblical record. Whether writing paraphrases of biblical texts or newly conceived hymns, the biblical materials infuse their work. It is as if the meaning and message of the Bible—its spirit and sometimes even its precise wording—are imbedded in their beings and through their memories work themselves out into their texts.

ii) The writers also exhibit an immersion in and knowledge of the world's great literature and often its music as well. They have learned from those who have written poetry, and sometimes music, before them. They know the literature and are humble enough to be taught by it. Literature and music are more or less obvious in their educational preparation, and poets and composers are implied or actually mentioned on numerous occasions in the interviews.

iii) Finally, perhaps because they are so imbued with the biblical message, the writers exhibit a deep commitment to the world they live in, to its problems and needs, and to its people. They sense the pains and joys of our age and seek to speak the compelling word of the gospel in hymnic language for our day so that we who sing will find ourselves unconsciously saying, "Aha, that's exactly what I meant to say but could not find the words." Fred Pratt Green's "When in Our Music God Is Glorified" is a most obvious example of this, but there are many others. As to specific themes, the sweep of the biblical message can be found in these texts—the story of God's grace, judgment, fire, and love especially evident in Christ—expressed in large measure by ranging across the wide expanse of topics the church year covers. If one were to isolate from this wide expanse a characteristic recurring *Zeitgeist* of our age to which these writers return more than their forebears, it would be justice, peace, and allied concerns. This is not only in actual themes, but in the increasingly obvious care for inclusive language as the century progressed.

Themes

Hymn texts themselves are obviously a central concern of any topic related to hymnody. But this book has not been an analysis of texts so much as it has been a discussion of broad themes, concerns, and perspectives that have to do with hymnody in our time and place.

Our guests—the writers and the members of the roundtable—celebrate the "hymn explosion." They are quite pleased with its breadth. They prize the interest it has generated in biblical themes and in hymnody itself. They greet the break out of a "frozen repertory," to use Russell Schultz-Widmar's expression,[1] with joy. If you set some of their comments about what pleases and gratifies them into a long string, you sense the magnitude of what we are witnessing and how grateful the persons consulted in this book are for it:

"the liberation of hymnody in both range and expression";

"more adventurous, willingness to take risks";

"the renewed interest in hymnody";

"the tacit approval of a Scripturally-based and inspired hymnody which responds to the grace and glory of the Triune God";

"the discovery of kindred spirits with the same ideals and principles as mine, but expressed in their own styles which differ from writer to writer";

"the emergence of new writers";

"the sheer wealth of talent and energy being devoted to hymn writing";

"the sheer richness of what is being created";

"the remarkable diversity of quality";

"the output of excellence";

"the intentional relating of hymn texts to Scripture";

"global hymnody";

"forms beyond stanzaic ones";

"more use of inclusive language";

"more hymns on the human condition, e.g. hunger, … natural resources, … racism";

"the number of hymnals being produced;

"the number of congregations which are commissioning new texts and tunes";

"picking up neglected and forgotten themes";

"the return of hymn poetry to the common speech of ordinary people."

This is a remarkable list. If you isolate it from other comments the writers and round-table members make, you might think hymnody had reached a golden age of perfection. But alongside this effusively positive series, there is another more ominous set of concerns. The negative set is longer and includes comments like these:

"the repetitious kind of song which can excite a congregation without deepening understanding and affecting practice";

"the trite, chorus-type, shallow evangelical, musically, poetically, and theologically unadventurous material that is being propagated with great commercial zeal by status-quo Christians";

"our fast-food approach to the Gospel";

"facile other-worldly discipleship which is no discipleship";

"the rifle association at prayer";

"the apparent belief that anyone with a guitar can dash off a 'worship song' fit to be sung by a congregation to almighty God, without effort, consultation, or revision—and often without grammar, syntax, meter, or rhyme either";

"catering to the lowest common denominator of poetic and musical taste";

"forsaking the Bible as a standard";

"[reducing] intellectual growth to nursery-rhyme level";

"instead of satisfying the cry for bread, offering circus entertainment";

"triviality … confusion between the flag and the cross … racism, sexism, heterosexism … abuses of power … increase in world hunger … the scale of poverty and homelessness … authoritarian use of the Bible as a cudgel and rule book … denominational insularity, national insularity, uncritical acceptance of our economic order";

"the promulgation of praise choruses and other musical 'junk food' that trivializes the spiritual significance of sacred song";

"literalism, anti-aestheticism, and anti-intellectualism ... what is shoddy and superficial ... lack of musical and literary education";

"the excruciating banality, the hopeless flatness";

"androcentric language, imagery, and assumptions [of past hymnody which means] continued use must be questioned [coupled with] everyone who has passed freshman English trying to write new hymns, in which the heresy is matched only by the sheer insipity of the lines";

"lack of fear and trembling ... no humility, no repentance, no cross ... no transcendence, no mystery";

"exclusively 'upbeat' [music] in major keys ... absence of [hymns about] the shadow- or down-side of life";

"confusion between what is 'for private devotional purposes' and what is 'more appropriate for corporate worship' ";

"hymns used for political agendas";

"*cliché bombes* [and] *logicide*";

"hymnody as a business to be exploited."

This list of negatives is as overwhelming as the positive one, and it is hard to understand how the two could coexist. They seem light years apart, related to different worlds. They are.

There is a whole world of new life in hymnody which the people consulted in this book affirm. Simultaneously there is another world which they find appalling. That does not mean all the writers and roundtable members agree. To suggest such a thing would be ludicrous, for they represent a wide diversity of theological perspectives.

What is striking, however, is the consensus that seems to lie behind the diversity of theological opinions. For all their disagreements, what concerns the people in this book is anything less than our best efforts and treating Christianity as a product to be sold. They are appalled when hymnody becomes commercial jingles; when it is turned into trivia or junk food; when it is geared to the level of the lowest common denominator and exploited as an item for sale; when the beauty, awe, and mystery of the message is

186

removed; when the full reality of the gospel in its prophetic challenge and priestly comfort is denied; and when the full range of human joys and sorrows is reduced to a parody. What unites them is a concern to treat people with the respect the gospel makes clear they deserve, to give the church its song in faithful words that are worth singing, and to assume our best efforts are required in hymnody as in everything else.

More than best efforts are implied. A writer could conceivably expend his or her best efforts on manipulating people with cleverly-devised jingles. That turns hymnody into a manipulative tool. The people in this book take another view. They assume a hymn requires from the writer an honest effort to give expression to the faith so that we may honestly sing it. The point is not to superimpose a manipulative foreign object, even if it is well-intentioned.

There is a critical divide here. It is not fundamentally about hymnody, though it hides itself there. It is fundamentally about morality—about how we are to conduct ourselves and how we are to treat others. Our three deceased guests put things in perspective quite well. Martin Franzmann, in his discussion of doing what "I like" no matter what great hymnodists have taught us, says this.

> *To pit my piping, squeaking, little ego against all the good gifts God has given his church ... is worse than snobbery; it is ingratitude ... [One] can make music on a tin whistle to the Glory of God ... but God has given us so infinitely much more ... When [God] has given us all the instruments under heaven with which to sing his praises, then the tin-whistle is no longer humility but a perverse sort of pride.[2]*

Erik Routley, in his discussion of sentimentality which he defines as "taking a shortcut to sensation which bypasses responsibility," quotes Vaughan Williams' comment about good taste being a moral concern and then says this.

> *Failures of taste are ultimately failures of nerve; bad taste argues insecurity, competitiveness, and a lust for quick results. Walk on the water in that spirit and you'll sink.[3]*

And in the poignantly experiential words of Sylvia Dunstan,

> *I learned that structure (meter, rhyme, etc.) empowered the people's singing ... 'meaningful thoughts' in sloppy form are an impedi-*

*ment to the people's prayer, causing undue focus on the work itself,
rather than pointing to the worship of God.*[4]

We live in an age of "insecurity, competitiveness, and a lust for
quick results." The Christian gospel, however, knows a shalom
which wipes out all our hopeless attempts to be secure, celebrates
a life which is not about winning but losing one's life in the waters
of Baptism and the vocation it propels into the world, and perceives
quick results to be deep delusions when in God's sight "a thousand years are like yesterday when it is past." Christian hymnody is
related to the second set of realities, not the first set of mirages.

The question before the church as it completes this millennium
is whether it has the courage and compassion to sing its song with
all its challenge and comfort, or whether it will be co-opted by the
world of marketing, the obscenity of targeting people, and the per-
version of hymnody to these devious ends. The question is not the
world's question which we hear seeping more and more into the
church, namely, figuring out how to get as many bodies as possible to buy your product, as if such frenzy will sustain the church.
God will sustain the church, as promised. The question is whether
we will get the message straight and sing the song of Christian faith,
or whether we will pervert it to our own crooked designs no matter how well-intentioned they may be.

Books about hymnody are never "just" about hymnody, because
hymnody and its underlay of psalmody are always about the whole
of human life in all its barbarity and finesse against the backdrop
of God's gracious love and mercy. But this book is even less "just"
about hymnody because the writers here pose a central question
so forthrightly to the church. They have lived out their vocations as
good and faithful servants. Will we?

Notes

1. Russell Schultz-Widmar, "Hymnody in the United States Since 1950," *The Hymnal 1982 Companion,* ed. Raymond F. Glover (New York: Church Hymnal Corporation, 1990), I: 600.
2. Martin H. Franzmann, *Ha! Ha! Among the Trumpets* (St. Louis: Concordia Publishing House, 1966), pp. 95–96.
3. Erik Routley, *Church Music and the Christian Faith* (Carol Stream: Agape, 1987),
p. 96.
4. Sylvia Dunstan, *In Search of Hope and Grace* (Chicago: GIA, 1991), Preface.